Statebuilding

Statebuilding

Consolidating Peace after Civil War

Timothy D. Sisk

polity

First published in 2013 by Polity Press

Polity Press
65 Bridge Street
Cambridge CB2 1UR, UK

Polity Press
350 Main Street
Malden, MA 02148, USA

ISBN-13: 978-0-7456-6158-2
ISBN-13: 978-0-7456-6159-9(pb)

A catalogue record for this book is available from the British Library.

Typeset in 10.25 on 13 pt Scala
by Servis Filmsetting Ltd, Stockport, Cheshire
Printed and bound in Great Britain by the MPG Printgroup

The publisher has used its best endeavours to ensure that the URLs for external websites referred to in this book are correct and active at the time of going to press. However, the publisher has no responsibility for the websites and can make no guarantee that a site will remain live or that the content is or will remain appropriate.

Every effort has been made to trace all copyright holders, but if any have been inadvertently overlooked the publisher will be pleased to include any necessary credits in any subsequent reprint or edition.

For further information on Polity, visit our website: www.politybooks.com

Contents

About the Author

Timothy D. Sisk is Professor and Associate Dean for Research at the Josef Korbel School of International Studies, University of Denver, and an Associate Fellow of the Geneva Centre for Security Policy in Geneva, Switzerland. He specializes in the comparative politics of war-torn countries and international conflict management efforts in them.

His research focuses on democracy and governance and the management of conflict in deeply divided societies, especially those emerging from civil war. He has conducted extensive research consultancies on the role of international and regional organizations, particularly related to or for the United Nations, in peace operations, peacemaking, and peacebuilding.

Sisk is the author of *International Mediation in Civil Wars: Bargaining with Bullets* (Routledge, 2009) and *Democratization in South Africa: The Elusive Social Contract* (Princeton University Press, 1995). He is the editor of the 2012 edited volume, *Between Terror and Tolerance: Religion, Conflict, and Peacebuilding* (Georgetown University Press). Other recent books for which he is co-editor are: *From War to Democracy: Dilemmas of Peacebuilding* (with Anna Jarstad, Cambridge University Press, 2008) and *The Dilemmas of Statebuilding: Confronting the Contradictions of Postwar Peace Operations* (with Roland Paris, Routledge, 2009). He is a former editor of the journal of the Academic Council of the United Nations System (ACUNS), *Global Governance: A Review of Multilateralism and International Organizations*.

Prior to joining the University of Denver in 1998, Sisk was a Program Officer and Research Scholar in the Grant Program of the United States Institute of Peace and, prior to that, a professional staff member for United States Senator Dale Bumpers of Arkansas. He earned a PhD "with distinction" in political science from The George Washington University in 1992 and an MA in International Journalism (1984) and a BA in Foreign Service and German (1982) from Baylor University.

Preface

The Libyan civil war of 2011 – which ended with the bloody ousting of the longstanding autocratic regime of Col. Moammar Qadhafi – underscores that the end of civil war does not automatically lead to the consolidation of peace. Indeed, for more than 40 years, the dictator Qadhafi had systematically inhibited the capacities of formalized state institutions, and instead he ruled through family, tribal, and other personalistic ties in the form of a "General People's Committee." He maintained his coercive grip on society mostly through informal networks and loose militias and, with these and other clients (including international mercenaries), Qadhafi managed a "distributive state" based on crafty distribution of the country's vast oil rents (Vandewalle 2006). Thus, when he was gruesomely killed on October 20, 2011, at the hands of rebel fighters on the final battlefield of war in Sirte and the insurgent National Transitional Council (NTC) emerged fully victorious, only the first step of the struggle for peace in Libya had been won . . . for the rebels, there was really no state to inherit.

After the end of the civil war in Libya, the country started with no integrated military establishment, no professional civil service, few institutions of justice and the rule of law, and no local or decentralized government to deliver basic services. The transitional government operated in a vacuum of authority, and for some time anarchy reigned as pro-Qadhafi forces fled, mostly tribally based insurgent militias took to the streets, and the Libyan state essentially ceased to function.[1]

After the victory over the loyalist forces, it was clear that an urgent yet long-term requirement was the need to build a new core pillar of the state, from the disparate elements of the revolutionary forces: the security forces.

Equally pressing in the immediate post-war moment, however, was the need to engage in a political process to legitimize the victorious rebel regime through rapid elections that could give the NTC a formal, legal basis as the custodians of the Libyan state. In June 2012, Libyans did go to the polls in, remarkably, mostly free elections (with the exception of eastern Libya, and especially the city of Benghazi, where violence and boycott threats disrupted the poll) to elect a new assembly that would serve as both an interim government and as a constitution-making body – the National Congress – as a process through which the state would be reconceived and reformed and a new social contract negotiated. Following the elections, outgoing United Nations envoy Ian Martin, head of the UN Support Mission in Libya (UNSMIL), addressing the UN Security Council in July 2012, after the elections, continued to put the focus in Libya on the long task of statebuilding:

> There is no underestimating the challenges and the expectations which the new government will face. Foremost among those is security – the issue which all agree was uppermost in the minds of voters. Contrary to some reporting, Libya's revolutionary brigades do not seek to remain in separate existence and to challenge state authority, but a government with full legitimacy and a longer time-horizon has been awaited to address their future. Libya's citizens overwhelmingly want the rule of law to prevail, in a weapons-free environment, where police respond to crime, and only state authorities arrest and detain suspects. Where local conflicts erupt, they want the rapid deployment of neutral, trusted security forces to maintain peace while underlying causes are addressed. Especially in the South, they want Libya's borders to be secured against the trafficking of persons, drugs and weapons.[2]

The challenge of stability in post-war Libya is reflective of a broader realization in post-civil war countries that state-building is the *telos* (or end goal) of consolidating peace. The statebuilding approach puts the social contract between citizen and the state at the forefront of long-term efforts to create the conditions for the management of conflicts within societies and for the provision of public goods necessary for their prosperity. In practice, this means focusing on the ability of the state to rule with authority or to provide internal security across its territory, to have the capacity to implement the rule of law, provide justice, deliver essential services needed for development, and enjoy the legitimacy that emanates from its being responsive to citizen demands. This book is about the global governance regime that emerged in the 1990s and through into the 2000s and 2010s based on the international efforts to consolidate peace after civil wars.

I would first like to thank Dr Louise Knight of Polity Press for suggesting the need for this book on statebuilding for the series on "War and Conflict in the Modern World." Her instigation is very much the inspiration for putting proverbial pen to paper on a topic that is much debated, but often with little conceptual clarity or an appreciation for the practical difficulties of the statebuilding enterprise. Together with David Winters at the Press, they have been exceedingly helpful (and patient!) as this book has come together. I am particularly grateful to two anonymous reviewers of an early draft of the text, and their insightful comments and helpful suggestions were absolutely invaluable in so many ways.

During 2007–2009, I was a consultant to the United Nations Development Program Bureau for Crisis Prevention and Recovery, when I worked closely with their seasoned and senior practitioners on the statebuilding themes from a UNDP perspective. Especially critical in furthering insights and guidance on statebuilding has been the always engaging and enlightening work in partnership with Senior Governance Advisor Eugenia Piza-Lopez and program specialist Dr Jago Salmon, together with countless UNDP practitioners who shared their experiences, frustrations, and successes on the front line of the statebuilding endeavors in the research work for the UNDP. My impression from working with the UNDP professionals is reflected in this book in many ways, and I am grateful for the opportunity to have learned and worked with such dedicated, committed, and most impressive international public servants.

I am also grateful to the Carnegie Corporation of New York for their support of two projects on statebuilding, both with Professor Roland Paris of the University of Ottawa; in particular, the Corporation supported a two-year, multifaceted research project on "Sustainable Approaches to Statebuilding" through which much of the research on this project was conducted. Particularly, at the Carnegie Corporation, I am grateful to Dr Stephen J. Del Rosso, Jr, for his personal support of this work and the broader program there on states at risk; many of the works cited in this book are the products of the Corporation's grant-making in this area. The Henry Luce Foundation's Initiative on Religion and International Affairs has graciously supported my research on divided societies and religious bodies and movements as informal institutions that are part and parcel of the debates on social cohesion reflected in chapter 4.

While I am deeply indebted to each of these supporters of my research on statebuilding, the views reflected herein are my own.

Timothy D. Sisk
Denver, Colorado
September 20, 2012

Abbreviations

CCA	Common Country Assessment
CEDAW	Convention on the Elimination of Discrimination against Women
CICIG	International Commission against Impunity in Guatemala
CPA	Comprehensive Peace Agreement (Sudan)
DDR	Disarmament, Demobilization, and Reintegration
DESA	Department of Economic and Social Affairs (United Nations)
DFID	Department for International Development (United Kingdom)
DPA	Development Partnership Administration (India)
DRC	Democratic Republic of Congo
EITI	Extractive Industries Transparency Initiative
EPRDF	Ethiopian People's Revolutionary Democratic Front
EUFOR	European Union Force (Bosnia)
FAO	Food and Agriculture Organization
FARC	Revolutionary Armed Forces of Colombia
FDI	Foreign Direct Investment
FDLR	Democratic Forces for the Liberation of Rwanda
FNL	Front for National Liberation (Burundi)

ICC	International Criminal Court
ICSS	International Commission on State Sovereignty
IDDRS	Integrated Disarmament, Demobilization and Reintegration Standards
IDEA	International Institute for Democracy and Electoral Assistance
IFOR	Implementation Force (Bosnia)
INGO	International Non-governmental Organization
ISF	Internal Security Forces (Lebanon)
LRA	Lord's Resistance Army (Uganda)
MDG	Millennium Development Goals
MONUSCO	United Nations Organization Stabilization Mission in the DRC
NATO	North Atlantic Treaty Organization
NGO	Non-governmental Organization
NTC	National Transitional Council (Libya)
OECD-DAC	Organization for Cooperation and Development Development Cooperation Directorate
OQR	Office of the Quartet Representative
PKK	Kurdish Workers Party
PR	Proportional Representation
PRT	Provincial Reconstruction Team
R2P	Responsibility to Protect
RENAMO	Mozambique National Resistance Organization
SFOR	Stabilization Force (Bosnia)
SNTV	Single Non-transferable Vote
SPLA	Sudan People's Liberation Army
SSR	Security Sector Reform
UCDP	Uppsala Conflict Data Program
UK	United Kingdom

UN	United Nations
UNAMID	United Nations Hybrid Mission in Darfur
UNDP	United Nations Development Program
UNEP	United Nations Environment Program
UNHCR	United Nations High Commissioner for Refugees
UNMIL	United Nations Mission in Liberia
UNMIN	United Nations Mission in Nepal
UNOCI	United Nations Operation in Côte d'Ivoire
UNODC	United Nations Office of Drugs and Crime
UNPROFOR	United Nations Protection Force (Bosnia)
UNSC	United Nations Security Council
UNSCOL	United Nations Special Coordinator for Lebanon
UNSMIL	United Nations Support Mission in Libya
USAID	United States Agency for International Development
WDR	World Development Report (World Bank)

Introduction

Following civil war, statebuilding is the creation or recovery of the authoritative, legitimate, and capable governance institutions that can provide for security and the necessary rule-of-law conditions for economic and social development. State capacities and governance capabilities are essential: while there is good reason to foster reconciliation at the societal level, ultimately the extent of peace consolidation is based on the building of a state that is socially accepted as a legitimate, accountable arbiter of social differences and a provider of critical public goods. Statebuilding has become an overarching concept to security and development in fragile states that envisages the improvement in governance institutions and processes at the national and local level as a way to channel and manage social conflicts away from the battlefield or streets and into regularized processes of non-violent resolution of social conflict through professional public administration, elections and parliamentary politics, and through participation and voice of citizens.

From the perspectives of outsiders, like the United Nations and multilateral and bilateral development partners, who seek to support post-war recovery through peacekeeping interventions and through development aid, the statebuilding approach takes advantage of the windows of opportunity that post-war transitions present to recreate or reform the state to prevent the recurrence of conflict and to promote human development in often deeply unequal or poor countries.[1]

This ambitious goal raises the principal question this book addresses: How can external engagement in post-war countries help build authoritative, capable, and legitimate states as a strategic approach to peace consolidation, thereby creating an enabling environment for development and democracy to mitigate the underlying drivers of conflict in the long run?

In this book, I argue that the contemporary statebuilding approach, and its concomitant areas of policy and practice, encapsulates the teleological end-state of international efforts to consolidate peace after civil war. However, the international community's approach – particularly by leading human rights, norm-driven actors such as the United Nations – must balance the lofty goal of "local ownership" of statebuilding processes with an explicit and sometimes very assertive liberal interventionist agenda of promoting a human rights-based approach to development and to democracy. While statebuilding *is* in theory the route to peace consolidation in situations of fragility, this enterprise can only be successful into the twenty-first century if the state that is built is one that is able to advance human rights-based development for the poorest and most marginalized sections of society, and a state that is built on a democratic social contract that links state legitimacy to participation and accountability by the people. International intervention for statebuilding is transformative, as many traditional and war-time informal institutions of governance persist, and outside actors must sometimes act with resolve and fortitude to advance international norms and standards of human rights and democracy.

Civil War and Post-War Fragility

Civil wars within states present global problems: as in Libya, they often see gross crimes against humanity in the form of attacks on civilians and near-genocidal killing; moreover, conflicts spill over with deleterious effects on neighboring states and regions, and they present man-made humanitarian emergencies that prompt international intervention to protect civilians and deliver relief (Wheeler 2000; Barnett 2011). Consequently, civil wars are at the forefront of the international security and development agendas into the twenty-first century. With the rise in the prevalence of internal conflicts that began in the post-Cold War era, and the fragile states and societies they leave behind, post-civil war statebuilding has risen to the very top of the international peace and security agenda. From top-level priorities at the United Nations, to global humanitarian non-governmental organizations (NGOs) such as Save the Children, to the National Security Strategy of great powers such as the United States, countries that are vulnerable to armed conflict are an ever-present threat to international peace and security. Statebuilding has equally come to the top of global development agendas with the realization that progress in development is inhibited by conflict, and that fragile and conflict-affected countries are precisely those that are not making progress toward the 2000–15 Millennium Development Goals (MDGs).[2]

While civil wars in faraway places do not necessarily pose direct security threats to the great powers such as the United States, they do present global deep-seated humanitarian challenges and indirect security challenges emanating from lawlessness or the effects of disorder (Patrick 2011). Consequently, in the last 20 years, the problem of internal conflict has precipitated the evolution of a broader system of international and regional response mechanisms by the leading states in the international system, the United Nations, regional organizations, multilateral and bilateral development aid agencies, and global civil society organizations to prevent and manage the effects of conflict and to build peace in wartorn countries. At the UN, as an outcome of the so-called

High-level Panel on Threats, Challenges, and Change, a major institutional shift occurred with the creation of the UN Peacebuilding Commission, the Peacebuilding Support Office, and the UN Peacebuilding Fund.

In responding to the problems that civil wars pose to global peace and security, the international community has turned its attention beyond short-term, crisis-response remedies such as humanitarian intervention, peacemaking (negotiating peace agreements; see Crocker et al. 2004), and peacekeeping, to long-term approaches that emphasize direct efforts to build state capacities in post-war contexts: *statebuilding*. In the wake of war, the root causes that underlie the turn to conflict in the first place are often inadequately addressed. These conflict-related legacies continue to have a detrimental effect on the population's safety, livelihoods, and opportunities for development. In sum, without progress on statebuilding and a new social contract, war-torn countries may well become trapped in vicious cycles of conflict: one of the most robust and recurrent findings from scholarly research presented in this book is that countries that experience civil war are more likely to fall victim to conflict in the future (see chapter 1).

Today, nearly 60 mostly post-war states out of 193 in the international system, populated by more than 1.5 billion people, are considered "fragile" or vulnerable to debilitating violence that in turn undermines prospects for development (World Bank 2011). The Organization for Development Cooperation-Development Coordination Directorate (OECD-DAC), the club of mostly Western donor agencies, defines fragility with this carefully honed definition: "States are fragile when state structures lack political will and/or capacity to provide the basic functions needed for poverty reduction, development and to safeguard the security and human rights of their populations."[3] The conflict trap of fragility at the societal level is in turn fueled and reinforced by weak, inept, or corrupt governments that fail to deliver basic security or essential services such as education, health care, or water and sanitation, the essential elements of long-term development. Because the aftermath of war leaves countries highly vulnerable to renewed or recurrent cycles of crisis conflict, they are today commonly and collectively – and sometimes contentiously – referred to as the "fragile states."[4]

In addition, these fragile countries will face enormous new economic and social pressures in the years ahead, and climate change, scarcity, and inequality may come together to fuel new wars in the future (United Nations Environment Program, UNEP, 2004).[5] There are good reasons to be concerned that future global shifts such as the effects of climate change will lead to new climate-induced conflicts prompted by migration, localized scarcity conflicts, rapid urbanization, and group-based inequalities (Hegre et al. 2009). Indeed, influential observers once in the United States government have argued that fragile states will continue to be a global security concern well into the twenty-first century (Krasner and Pascual 2005).[6]

Consolidating Peace: From Peacebuilding to Statebuilding

In the now-landmark 1992 Agenda for Peace, a document drafted by then UN Secretary-General Boutros Boutros-Ghali following the first-ever summit at the level of heads of state of the UN Security Council (UNSC), the term "peacebuilding" was coined as an initial approach to address the problems that post-civil war countries face (Boutros-Ghali 1992). Peacebuilding – preventing the recurrence of conflict and beginning to address its root causes – is primarily about implementing peace agreements and fostering reconciliation (Sandole 2011). Statebuilding, as such, is a specific approach to peacebuilding that sees improvements in government capacities to deliver on security and development aims as a long-term linchpin to consolidating peace and solidifying the institutions and processes of governance to create the conditions for societies to sustainably develop and prosper on their own. In this vein, statebuilding is a complementary approach to peacebuilding, and while they are not synonymous (and can even be contradictory when short-term stabilization leaves warlords and militias empowered, which may work against long-term consolidation of state authority), the peacebuilding and statebuilding terms are in many ways aimed at addressing the same challenges in post-war contexts (Wyeth and Sisk 2009; Rocha Menocal 2009), albeit perhaps with slightly different time horizons.

Historically, the formation of states and the centralization of governance authority in the state were essentially internal or endogenous processes through which dominant elites expanded power and authority and developed capacities through consent (e.g., through taxation and other revenue raising) to eventually become the sole source of legitimate use of coercion in a country (following Weber and others; see chapter 2). States were formed and consolidated, in large part, in response to internal threats and internal grand projects to construct nations under single governmental authority. In this sense, statebuilding is a highly political process through which national-level government institutions prevail over rebel groups, warlords, and hereditary authority (such as religious authorities, chiefs, and traditional leaders), in a consolidated territory, and which is recognized internationally as enjoying legal sovereignty. The consolidation of state power in the Western world, and in countries like China, took centuries of often internal violent struggles between the would-be state and its contenders – criminals and warlords, insurgents, separatists, and insurgents – as well as external wars with aggressive external foes such as neighbors or would-be colonizers.

Over time, the state as a sovereign emerged through the gradual expansion of capacities: protecting the state from outside threats, revenue raising and spending on citizens in an implicit exchange relationship, institutional development of ministries, agencies, and regulatory bodies, and formation and reformation of justice-providing structures into a rationalized, legal order, approximating the consolidated states that govern much of the globe today. Similarly, many countries evolved over time from authoritarian regime types to democratic states, a non-linear process which is still ongoing even though there are more democracies in the world today than ever before; some, such as Amartya Sen, have convincingly argued that democracy has become a "universal value" (1999).

Today, statebuilding in fragile states is mostly endogenous, as before, but it also involves no small measure of external intervention and post-war assistance to aid post-war regimes to consolidate authority. Thus, statebuilding today has an expanded and arguably different connotation, reflecting both internal, domestic dynamics of post-war governance and outside military intervention (for example, through peacekeeping) and development aid. "Statebuilding" in contemporary parlance – sometimes known as "international statebuilding" to reflect the prominent role that outsiders play in such processes – is very much about the interactions of internal *and* external or international efforts to essentially expedite and indeed shape endogenous processes with external involvement to end wars, primarily through military interventions, and through post-war development aid flows and technical assistance (human resource expertise). In today's world, international actors seek to shape the type of state that is built to ensure domestic alignment with international norms, such as the rights of women, minorities, or vulnerable elements in the population such as those with disabilities . . . and through norms that suggest a global right to good governance and democracy (see chapter 6).

It is in this sense that statebuilding has emerged since the late 1990s and into the present century as a principal strategic perspective that creates common ground between security and development agendas for consolidating peace in countries emerging from civil war. From a security perspective, statebuilding is the end goal of efforts to stabilize war-torn countries and create a sole, legitimate authority that can be held accountable internally and internationally. From a development perspective, statebuilding sees the need for an authoritative government under the rule of law as a precondition for gains in economic growth and in human development.

The conviction underlying the modern statebuilding concept is that outsiders *can* assist essentially domestic processes of statebuilding. The statebuilding approach is guided by an acknowledgment that states are built mostly from within and that international assistance must depart from the principle of "local ownership" in trying to assist statebuilding efforts after civil war. Jean-Marie Guéhenno, Chair of the Secretary-General's Senior Advisory Group for the Review of International Civilian Capacities (described in chapter 7) asserts that "international assistance has to identify, protect and nurture latent national capabilities, in short, that it must build on what is already there, not start from a blank slate."[7]

This dedication to the principle of local ownership, however well-intentioned, is fraught with problems. Local ownership, a concept with its origins in approaches to community-level development, is difficult in practice when outsiders meet the realities of post-war environments, where the scope of the challenge of humanitarian catastrophe and recovery is immense, where local ruling elites may act in a predatory way, and where there is deep social distrust of the state to begin with. These vexatious questions have led scholars to evaluate the statebuilding enterprise in terms of a set of dilemmas at the intersection of the international system and the messy realities of local context (these questions are considered more fully in chapter 3). These dilemmas are especially acute when international interveners must engage and negotiate with non-state armed actors whose commitment to peace is often questionable (Henri Dunant Center 2010).

Statebuilding is a complex and problematic process. In many cases, statebuilding is a vexatious effort because elites at the top are often predatory or ethnically focused, state authorities are neglectful or inept, and there is little trust in these fledgling institutions; instead, security is provided (if at all) by traditional chiefs and clan leaders, armed militias and insurgents, or criminal networks, and development is stagnant with little hope for improved livelihoods. Although statebuilding is the common and often implicit goal of international organizations, development agencies, and transnational NGOs, there is little consensus about how international organizations or states acting alone, through external military interventions (to provide security) and aid instruments (to enable development), can conceivably accomplish such an ambitious and inherently political aim.

For outsiders, dilemmas of approach and action abound, approaches diverge, there is often little coherence and coordination among international entities (Paris 2009). Interventions are costly and sometimes indeterminate, and heavy-handed approaches by international interveners can backfire. Moreover, there are few clear answers to the core questions of how to avoid the risks in enabling state capacities – preventing states from being captured by predatory elites, ethnic factions, or leaders that turn out to be authoritarian – and how to effectively use aid to create the incentives for states that are accountable to their own people, not outsiders. And,

in the immediate aftermath of conflict, it may be more efficient and effective to deliver aid through informal networks,
such as religious organizations or faith-based NGOs, that
may not share international agendas on issues such as gender
equality. The debates about statebuilding play out in international organizations, today's great and emerging powers, and
most significantly in those societies struggling to create new
governments to meet security, development, and democracy
aspirations after war.

Thus, in the twenty-first century, statebuilding involves
a constant and perhaps unending search for an appropriate
balance between an endogenous, locally driven process that
is internally "owned" by the recognized government – and,
ostensibly, the "people" – and one in which international
actors assertively and without excuse advance global norms.
In short, statebuilding cannot be a value-neutral endeavor
based solely in the principle of "local ownership:" it should
have a clearly transformative agenda as well if the goal of universal peace and security is to be pursued.

About this Book

This book explores the challenges of civil war and the
responses that have emerged to try to reverse cycles of conflict
and underdevelopment through an emphasis on building the
capacity of post-war states to extend their autonomy, authority, capacity, and legitimacy. The challenges and dilemmas the
statebuilding approach presents are reflected in several critical questions that get at the heart of contemporary issues in
war and peace.

- How can a viable, functioning state be built in the aftermath
  of civil war as a strategic approach to consolidating peace in
  the long term?

- What are the conditions under which, in practice, governance reform in fragile countries can create the underlying
conditions that are needed for development – security, education, health care, water and sanitation, and livelihoods
– which in turn can reverse vicious cycles to help stimulate
a virtuous cycle of peace and development?
- How can outsiders constructively assist inherently domestic
processes of building the authority, legitimacy, and capacity
of states . . . especially when these post-war governments
are typically weak, captured, or corrupt?

The objective of this book is to introduce and explore prevailing concepts, discourse, debates, and dilemmas of
statebuilding. Drawing on scholarly and practitioner literatures and on a wide array of examples from every major
world region, the book introduces the reader to the strategic,
practical, and ethical issues in contemporary statebuilding.
Special topics considered in the book include issues such
as advancing women's rights and livelihoods, inclusion and
participation of marginalized and vulnerable groups, the role
of informal authorities such as tribal, clan, or religious leaders, and the opportunities and sometimes disappointment of
efforts to build local capacities.

The book presents some of the prevailing scholarly and
practitioner literatures on statebuilding to introduce the
reader to the principal themes and areas of practice now
found in international organizations, leading states, bilateral
and multilateral development aid agencies, and NGOs. There
is a strong reliance in these pages on the analysis and reflec
tion of various practitioners, as seen in the material drawn
from international organizations such as the UN and the
OECD-DAC, which have invested considerably in reflection
on lessons learned and on their analysis of both challenges
and solutions to the statebuilding conundrums. In general, I

have found the research methods and findings of these organizations to be genuine and robust, albeit with perhaps an institutional bias to present a more positive spin on their own roles and programs. On the other hand, I have also tried to include those voices – typically, scholars and advocacy groups – who have challenged the assumptions on which international organizations work and who have offered critical views of orthodox statebuilding approaches and practices.

The disadvantage of the methods employed here are that much of the present scholarship and policy reflection on these matters lacks a systematic way to ascertain how the 1.5 billion people who live in fragile countries see the role of the state and its authority, capacity, and legitimacy. For many, the state may in fact be a very distant reality that has little bearing on their security or their livelihoods. While some philanthropic foundations have begun to seed research that explores how those living in situations of insecurity or deprivation see the statebuilding efforts, there is little ability to generalize on popular views toward what are often global-level debates and processes that take place in faraway centers of international power or in capitals that are very distant from their own front-line realities of living in conditions of "fragility."

A second disadvantage may be that the scope of the topic is vast – from rebuilding Somalia's central state, to extending local government in Guatemala, to creating a "tax-mediated" social contract in Afghanistan – such that it is difficult within so few pages to go in depth into specific cases or to fully show the variance of context and culture. To mitigate this problem, I have sought to include reference to examples to allow the reader to go into greater depth in any particular example or country-level case study.

Chapter 1 presents the current context for the focus on statebuilding by introducing trends in armed conflict, violence, and state fragility in the twenty-first century. We begin by first looking at the pattern of armed conflicts and their termination since the end of the Cold War, and the security, humanitarian, and development challenges that post-war, fragile states pose to the international system. The chapter presents some of the leading theories on the underlying drivers of internal conflict and civil war in terms of their root causes, the ways in which patterns of war termination – military victory or negotiated settlement – affect the starting points for post-war recovery, and the consequences of conflict for the post-war period as a way to unpack the syndrome of fragility.

Chapter 2 defines and delineates conceptual approaches to statebuilding by exploring its origins in core theories of the state that emerged as a consequence of historical patterns in Western Europe, countries such as China, and statebuilding in post-colonial contexts. The statebuilding notion is grounded in the need for *authority* to enforce the rule of law, the need for a "tax-mediated social contract" between state and society, the *capacity* to govern in pursuit of providing for citizen or human security and in creating the conditions for economic and social development, and *legitimacy* through popular participation in terms of state–society relations.

In Chapter 3, I present some of the leading debates on the tension between international liberal order based on human rights and global norms and engagement in the messy realities of post-war countries – interventions which Roland Paris has thoughtfully termed a colonization-like *mission civilisatrice*, or a "civilizing mission" (2002). The chapter summarizes some of the scholarly and practitioner debates on contemporary approaches to statebuilding, and it highlights the dilemmas of action that emerge in complex international–domestic interactions. It grapples with how to conceptualize the notion of state autonomy, or the ability of a state to implement its own vision and goals, in the face of broad-based and sometimes heavy-handed international engagement. In many ways, these issues of the purpose and limits of international intervention are at the very heart of the transformation of the international system into the twenty-first century.

In chapters 4 through 6, the conceptual approach developed in chapter 2 organizes the subsequent analysis of the dimensions and practical tasks of statebuilding. Chapter 4 focuses on a first-order priority: the imperative of security and the consolidation and extension of state authority. It investigates the importance of a "security-first" perspective to statebuilding and the ways in which securing the state and extending its authority are the primary concerns for local protagonists and international interveners alike. In this chapter, I argue that security sector reform must be holistically conceptualized, and that other goals of statebuilding will prove elusive without security advances. The chapter explores the impetus for intervention by the international community – either through the UN, or in some cases by external military forces of leading states through "coalitions of the willing" – when states fail to effectively govern their territory and the vacuum or misuse of power leads to mass atrocities that pose broader security threats and humanitarian aid costs to the entire international community. Consolidating authority and realizing security are pursued through two mechanisms: disarmament, demobilization, and reintegration of armed, non-state forces such as rebel groups, and the restructuring and sometimes wholesale recreation of the security sector (armies and police forces). The chapter ends with a look at emerging approaches to security with a focus on community-level social cohesion and proliferating conflict management capacities at the local level.

Chapter 5 turns from security and authority to development and state capacity to deliver basic services. A critical objective of statebuilding is to create the conditions through which the state can foster development through the macroeconomic stability, taxation and fiscal management, and service delivery of essential public goods such as universal primary education. And, because a deep driver of fragility is competition over access to natural resources (such as export-related commodities like minerals or oil and gas), and over productive agricultural land, resource management and wealth sharing have become critical components of the statebuilding perspective. An immediate need is to address the plight of the desperately poor, or those suffering chronic poverty and acute insecurities such as lack of food, access to water and sanitation, and opportunities for livelihoods with dignity. Thus, I argue for a human rights-oriented approach to development, rather than a more narrow perspective that is principally focused on economic growth. This approach relates back to a core finding about conflict dynamics that injustice and inequality – so-called "relative deprivation," described in chapter 1 – are strong underlying drivers of violence and that the failure to attend to basic human needs for those whose rights are compromised can only create the conditions for future conflict. States today, equally, have obligations to provide basic or essential services that underpin development, such as education, health care, and clean water and sanitation.

Chapter 6 presents the argument that the most institutionalized and viable type of state is a democratic one that is inclusive and participatory, and that protects and promotes fundamental human rights. Because a state is only strong when it is based on mutually reinforcing state–society relations, statebuilding as such cannot be dissociated from the agendas of democracy building and advancement of human rights, particularly for women. Like other areas of statebuilding, however, there are problems and indeed deep dilemmas in efforts to promote democracy or to advance human rights in ways that actually entail societal transformation (Sisk 2008). Whether it is introducing electoral processes in countries with little experience in democracy, or in advancing rights of women in societies where traditions and cultures are antithetical to gender equality, fostering a democratic state – while a laudable long-term goal – is bedeviled by difficult and volatile political transitions and the need for dramatic social transformation to address deeply engrained historical inequalities along identity lines. These challenges of democracy building, however, should not be offered up as an excuse to sacrifice the goals of democracy and human rights in the belief that stability can be fostered first, or without them. Rather than trading off democracy for some elusive attempt to find "stability," international actors need to better understand and address the ways to infuse messy and sometimes violent processes of democracy building with a conflict prevention perspective.

The book concludes in chapter 7 with a discussion of the steps needed to create a better global "regime" – international and regional norms on governance and their implementation – to improve international efforts aimed at development and democratic governance in fragile states. What innovations in thinking and improvements in action are needed to create a more effective and enduring set of rules and norms, agreements and approaches, and operational implementation of the statebuilding agenda? The conclusion presents observations for further evolution of international norms and intervention to arrest state failure in the worst instances. In conclusion, it offers ways to improve the effectiveness of international development assistance to enable more locally owned statebuilding, where possible, and to balance genuine local ownership of the statebuilding process with the global norms, emphasizing a rights-based approach to human development and democracy.

CHAPTER ONE

Civil War and Post-War Fragility

The problem of violent conflict within countries – civil wars, inter-communal clashes, and one-sided repression by autocratic regimes that approach the level of mass atrocities – characterizes the principal threat to peace and security in the post-Cold War era and into the present age (Hewitt et al. 2010). Since the end of the Cold War in 1989 and into the twenty-first century, armed conflict primarily within countries – or, civil wars[1] – emerged as the principal, immediate threat to international peace and security. The internal armed conflicts of the 1990s, 2000s, and now into the 2010s, have well eclipsed prior concerns of interstate war that had so plagued the twentieth century (although some "dyads," such as between Iran and Israel, threaten to escalate into interstate war).

The "new wars" in the international system presented more-or-less new problems of how and when to intervene to mitigate the domestic and international consequences of armed conflict – and once engaged, how to exit.[2] Countries that have experienced internal armed conflict appear particularly vulnerable to conflict recurrence, either in the re-eruption of civil war or in patterns of violence and poverty that reflect the acute human insecurities that are found in the wake of conflict. These war-torn countries remain highly "fragile" at the state and societal levels: prone to political crises and violent episodes, crime and armed violence, chronic poverty, and the seeming inability to break out of conflict and poverty

traps. In these countries, the state often lacks the basic authority over its territory, the capacity to deliver essential security or
public services, and the legitimacy to address social problems
and to act decisively.

Scholars Frances Stewart and Graham Brown cogently
define fragile states as experiencing chronic gaps in their
authority (i.e., the presence of organized political violence),
in their ability to provide service entitlements (i.e., inadequate
delivery of basic education, water, etc.), and their deeply compromised legitimacy (i.e., limited support among the people)
(Stewart and Brown 2009). As we shall see, while Somalia –
without a formal, effective government since 1989 – may well
be the quintessential failed or fragile state, deeper analysis
suggests that even poorly governed middle-income countries
are subject to state failure and post-war fragility, as the examples of Libya or subsequently in Syria in 2011–12, attest. And,
while all countries (including highly developed Norway,
the UK, or the US) can see episodes of political or terrorist
violence, there is an appreciation that vulnerability to civil
war can be carefully measured along both state and societal
dimensions.

This chapter explores the various definitions and indeed
contested terrain around the concept and experiences of fragility in developing world countries. As Charles Tilly observes,
"despite the great place that war making occupied in the
making of European states, the old national states of Europe
almost never experienced the great disproportion between
military organization and all other forms of organization
that seems the fate of [post-colonial] client states throughout
the contemporary world" (1985: 186). The challenges and
dynamics of statebuilding today unfold in remarkably different contexts from those in prior historical epochs: post-war
countries, largely found in the deeply underdeveloped regions
of Africa, South Asia, Central America, and since 2011 in the

post-autocratic Middle East, typically face an array of challenges to state authority, from transnational criminal groups to "spoiler" rebel factions to ongoing social tensions (often along identity lines).

The chapter explores the number and extent of countries with recent experiences of civil war in the international system, critically evaluates efforts to measure insecurity and underdevelopment, and highlights the syndromes or patterns of mutually reinforcing, "vicious cycles" of insecurity and underdevelopment captured by the fragility language. Without an initial, clear setting of the scene in which contemporary statebuilding occurs, we cannot understand the ways in which outsiders may begin to remediate the problems of fragility through aiding processes of statebuilding.

Civil Wars into the Twenty-first Century: Trends and Patterns

What countries today are characterized by fragility, and what are the consequences for security and development? As mentioned above, despite the persistence of international war between states (for example, recently involving Eritrea and Ethiopia in the early 2000s or the Israel and Lebanon/ Hezbollah conflict in 2006), since the end of the Cold War, wars between states are rare and generally limited in scope.[3] From 1989 to 2010, there were 133 armed conflicts globally. Of these conflicts, 93 percent were internal to states.[4] Conflicts over borders and self-determination, between ethnically based political forces, and violence stemming from fights over scarce natural resources (such as oil, precious metals, or diamonds) pose the most immediate, directly injurious threats to international peace and security. As James Fearon has shown, civil wars tend to last longer than international wars with an average duration since 1945 of more than ten years (2006).[5]

The Uppsala Conflict Data Program reports that in 2010, there were active around the world some 30 conflicts between governments and rebel groups in 25 countries that meet their definition of "armed conflict" (more than 25 battle-related deaths) (Themnér and Wallensteen 2011). Violent armed conflict and high levels of armed violence affect nearly a third of countries across the globe or nearly 60 states in the international system. This includes those countries that in 2013 are experiencing civil war (e.g., Afghanistan, Colombia, the Democratic Republic of Congo, Pakistan, Syria, Sudan and South Sudan, and Somalia to name a few) and those that have recently seen peace agreements but which, observers readily agree, could see new or renewed conflict (e.g., Burundi, Liberia, Libya, Nepal, and Sierra Leone).

The conflicts are "mostly" internal because no war today is wholly internal and without effects on neighbors and the international system more broadly. Today, conflicts across borders are seen often in cross-border incursions to deal with state collapse, such as Kenya's intervention in Somalia in 2011 to take on the Islamist *al-Shabaab*, which seeks to conquer territory and create an extremist Islamic state in the country; Kenya intervened when militants from the group kidnapped Westerners on Kenyan soil. In another example, the rebel Ugandan Lord's Resistance Army (LRA), after being defeated within the territory of Uganda in its war against the government, slipped into neighboring DRC, the Central African Republic, and South Sudan, menacing communities as a marauding band of murderous thieves committing atrocities throughout central Africa. In West Africa, in the wake of the civil wars in Sierra Leone, Liberia, and Côte d'Ivoire, transnational criminal organizations have emerged as challengers to the fledgling post-war governments (and as "soft" threats to European countries when such criminal organizations use their West Africa base to infiltrate into Europe).

Moreover, it is equally appropriate to see many contemporary civil wars as "regional conflict complexes," a phrased coined by scholars Peter Wallensteen and Margareta Sollenberg in the late 1990s to describe the linkages among conflicts in regional settings such as West Africa, the Horn of Africa, or Southwest Asia, in which conflict dynamics are intertwined across state borders (1998). Consequently, there is a burgeoning literature on the "internationalization" of conflict and the cross-border ties through which many conflict groups derive critical moral and material support (Wolff 2003). In many instances – such as Afghanistan, Kashmir, Sri Lanka, former Yugoslavia, Rwanda, and Burundi, to name just a few – conflicts were fueled and complicated by strong identity bonds that link groups across borders, for example. The 2012 upsurge in conflict between the Turkish government and the Kurdish Workers Party (PKK) rebel group has much to do with new capacities for the Kurdish resistance to organize given the autonomy granted to the Kurds in the post-Saddam constitution in Iraq.

And civil wars tend to draw in international intervention. The case of Kenya in Somalia in 2011 cited above, and other examples, such as NATO intervention in the Libyan civil war in 2011 in an effort to prevent a humanitarian catastrophe, demonstrate that international engagement in civil war continues to be common and most internal wars have an international dimension. It may well be that successful international intervention with the result of affecting regime change (whether by a great power, in the case of Iraq in 2003), or the fall of Qadhafi in 2011, has caused powers such as Russia and China to back away from norms of intervention . . . perhaps fearing that their own internal protests could spiral out of control. The principle of international intervention to halt suffering and gross violations of human rights is now being tested out on the streets of Syria, and (as I discuss in the conclusion), the responsibility to protect also implies a responsibility to rebuild the state after conflict.

The number of armed conflicts globally has steadily declined in recent years as war terminations have tended to exceed war onsets, such that the overall downward slope in the frequency of armed conflict remains in a downward direction since the peak in 1992. However, today a new grey zone exists in internationalized internal armed conflicts, for example when the government of a state such as the United States is engaged in protracted conflict with non-state actors, such as *al-Qaida* in Iraq, Somalia, or Yemen, or against the Taliban in Afghanistan and its shadowy armed criminal network allies in neighboring Pakistan. The Uppsala Conflict Data Program (UCDP) has addressed this type of conflict by referring to them as "internationalized internal conflicts" (see note 1 for a web link to the definitions used by the UCDP).

The overall downward trend in the frequency of such wars reveals patterns that go against the conventional wisdom of a world ablaze with deadly violence and unending wars. This "world ablaze" view is partially true – almost any given day a deadly civil war is at the top of the international news. However, scholarly measurement of armed conflict frequency and intensity reaffirms the assertion that, overall, the world is becoming a more peaceful place. This decline is commonly and sometimes controversially attributed to the increased effectiveness of the international community to facilitate peace settlements though peacemaking, or the capacity of the international community to coax the parties into a peace agreement.[6] Progress has been palpable: by 2005, wars had decreased by 60 percent from an earlier peak in 1992 to the lowest level of warfare on the globe since the 1950s.

In 2010, the most devastating conflicts in terms of lives lost in armed conflict were found in Afghanistan, Pakistan, Somalia, and Iraq; new "onsets" such as the 2011 conflict in

Libya or the civil war that emerged in Syria at the end of 2011 and into 2012 underscores that new wars can erupt rapidly, including in middle-income countries where authoritarian regimes have brutally repressed demands for democracy and greater accountability. Thus, the data on conflict trends must always be analyzed cautiously in making broader inferences about whether armed conflict within states could, over time, become as infrequent as international conflict between states. If the international community can better help countries emerging from conflict not relapse into violence – i.e., through statebuilding – then the overall eradication of war could well be a realizable objective in the century.

The problem of the recurrence of conflict in those countries that have experienced civil wars in recent years is evident, and this fact has driven the international agenda to ensure a long-term engagement to consolidate peace in war's wake. Hewitt et al. report that:

> Strikingly, of the 39 different conflicts that became active in the last 10 years, 31 were conflict recurrences – instances of resurgent, armed violence in societies where conflict had largely been dormant for at least a year. Only eight were entirely new conflicts between new antagonists involving new issues and interests. These sobering numbers serve as a reminder that many of the destabilizing dangers of the conflict syndrome ... continue to pose serious challenges during the post-conflict phase, underscoring the urgency for identifying appropriate policy responses during post-conflict reconstruction (2010: 1).

The perhaps utopian view of a world free from armed conflict can only be realized if the international community can solve the perplexing problems involved in preventing new violence from recurring in putatively "post-conflict" countries.[7]

Underlying Drivers of Fragility

If the international community is to understand the con-textual dynamics of consolidating peace after war and statebuilding for sustaining the peace, it must proceed with a deep understanding of the underlying drivers of fragility that leave countries vulnerable to recurrent cycles of violence. And it must improve the way it goes about assessing local contexts to find variation and specificity in these situations.[8] Especially, there must be an understanding of the ways in which the state, as a prize in a violent competition, has been at times a party to conflict. States often exacerbate conflict dynamics through unequal public policies; in some instances, has been captured by a dominant class or group, or has repressed the rights and disabled the livelihoods of vulnerable minorities. Understanding the deep drivers of fragility and the role of the competition for the state in driving fragility is a necessary starting point for understanding the extent to which, and how, the international community can help build states to mitigate these deep-seated structural conditions that are reflected in state power.

In the very worst contexts, civil war yields governments that are unable to respond adequately to the needs of their citizens; because civil war is usually over control of the state or seces-sion of territory from the state, the state's ability to govern is often the first victim in a violent struggle. I. William Zartman insightfully defines post-war state failure in these words:

> The basic functions of the state are no longer performed. As the decision-making center of government, the state is paralyzed and inoperative: laws are not made, order is not preserved, and societal cohesion is not enhanced. As a symbol of identity, it has lost its power of conferring a name on its people and a meaning to their social action. As a terri-tory, it is no longer assured security and provisionment by a

central sovereign organization. As the authoritative political institution, it has lost its legitimacy, which is therefore up for grabs, and so has lost the right to command and conduct public affairs (1995: 5).

Barnett Rubin (2003) emphasizes that causal accounts for civil war and ultimately recurring fragility are to be found conjointly at international, national, and local levels of analysis. Some causes of fragility can be found in the very structure of the international system – such as the historical legacy of colonial-era borders and the dysfunctional post-colonial states that reflected the interests and power of erstwhile colonizers, or globalization-induced growth of socio-economic inequalities[9] – while other drivers are found at national and local or micro- levels.

At both national and local levels, theories of the state play a central role in leading causes-of-conflict theories. For example, Paul Brass argues that in ethnically diverse societies the state is a prize, and that the role of the state in balancing ethnic relations is a pivotal variable in more peaceful or more violent outcomes.[10] The close fit between causes of conflict analysis and the problem of exclusion of key groups from state power raises a number of questions about how state weakness and ultimately failure are related to the persistent exclusion of key segments of the population from representation and influence in the state, and the role that state-perpetuated inequalities play in social conflicts driven by frustration and a deep sense of identity-based injustices. It is for this reason that later in the book I argue that inclusion of formerly excluded and marginalized populations is, and should be, a central focus of contemporary statebuilding.

Thus a key predictor of conflict vulnerability within countries is bad leadership, particularly predatory elites: corrupt rulers bent on rent-seeking (as in Sierra Leone prior to its civil war),[11] narrow ethnic ruling cliques (as in Syria), and military-industrial regimes in which the military runs vast industrial enterprises (as in Myanmar). Countries poorly governed by authoritarian elites, or by corrupt and predatory regimes that fail to deliver security and prosperity for their people, are deeply vulnerable to challenges from beleaguered societies . . . as the riotous and sometimes violent challenges to corrupt rulers in the 2011 Arab Spring attests.

Robert Bates' work on post-colonial Africa shows how independence-era elites – claiming a mantle of legitimacy based on the politics of liberation – were subsequently able to seize the state and act in an essentially corrupt predatory way, which in large part explains persistent fragility among many countries in the region (2008). Bates artfully shows in analysis of cases such as Rwanda, Sudan, Liberia, and the Democratic Republic of Congo that the leaders of poor states, with weak accountability mechanisms, used their hold on power to accumulate as much as they could for themselves as quickly as they could . . . they had little incentive to build a functioning state. As will be argued in chapter 4, this perspective of elite incentives for statebuilding informs much of the contemporary approaches to political economy analysis and capacity building in post-war countries.

Equally, and perhaps related, there are those who emphasize primarily structural economic conditions as a root cause of conflict, particularly greedy, predatory elites (such as Collier et al.'s 2003 *Breaking the Conflict Trap*). Economic approaches emphasize the presence of abundant natural resources (to include land), access to "lootable" goods – diamonds, oil, timber – and the role of greedy conflict entrepreneurs in forging insurgencies to capture these resources. Economic dependence on single or especially valuable commodities derived from natural resources can in fact enable armed conflicts and may lengthen their duration, especially when desperate governments or rebel forces can capture local access to critical markets or chokepoints in global trade (Cramer 2002). Capture of natural resources, especially of high-value oil and gas reserves or precious primary commodities, is a strong underlying driver of distributive conflicts that have over time erupted into violent conflict. Infamously, diamonds were at the heart of the conflict in Sierra Leone, which witnessed some of the most horrible atrocities that occurred at the dawn of the twenty-first century; for this reason, statebuilding in post-war Sierra Leone has been focused on creating a new framework for the mining, export, and labor conditions in the mines, and in a new framework for the state to fairly allocate diamond export earnings.[12]

Underlying environmental conditions may portend scarcity, competition over land and water, or resource exploitation conflicts. For example, some – including UN Secretary-General Ban Ki-moon – have referred to the Darfur war as the first climate change-induced conflict, suggesting that international systemic variables must also be part of the equation.[13] Many analysts suggest that many civil wars today play out primarily at local or sub-national regional levels in countries already experiencing high conditions of vulnerability to conflict (and to natural disasters). There is concern, and some evidence, that environmental scarcity and change may well be the root cause of local and sometimes national-level violence and fragility (United Nations Environment Program 2004).

It is not just scarcity that induces conflict, however; violence may also erupt in conditions of "plenty" over the distribution of rents from natural resources. Many contemporary civil wars have their roots in so called distributive inequality conflict. Conflict in countries or contexts such as Aceh (Indonesia), Mindanao (the Philippines), Nigeria's Delta Region, and Bolivia's tensions in recent years have been driven in large part by exclusion of local peoples from access to rents from natural resource extraction when revenues are controlled by either central government or transnational corporations (Ballentine and Sherman 2003).

But economics alone does not fully explain vulnerabilities to violence. Ethnic enmity, religious intolerance, or other identity-based social structures (e.g., tribal and clan systems) can also be strong drivers of conflict, especially when economic opportunity and identity overlap. Psychological factors in conflict escalation emphasize the seemingly inherent nature of group-oriented identities, combined with narratives of injustice or indignities that can become pathologies of ethnic or sectarian conflict.[14] Snyder and Jervis have shown how the "ethnic security dilemma," or mutual fears and perceptions of vulnerability and imminent danger can lead to offensive action, particularly in the context of volatile political transitions (Snyder and Jervis 1999; see also Lake and Rothchild 1996); this pattern of the ethnic security dilemma seems to be unfolding in the case of Syria in 2012, where conflict between rebels and the regime has taken on a distinctly sectarian dimension.[15] Fragility is a consequence not just of economic conditions alone, but in their interaction with social structures that can give rise to group-based grievances and identity-based challenges to the state (Horowitz 1985, Jenkins and Gottlieb 2007, Stewart 2008, Gurr 1993, 2000).

Economic and social divisions within countries are often exacerbated by the state, yielding political economy relationships of "horizontal inequalities" (Stewart n.d.). Resource-driven conflicts have been those that are related to scarcity, and those that are related to the "resource curse," in which natural endowments of high-valued commodities lead to conflicts over access, or from frustration driven by marginalization or exclusion from the revenue that returns from these resources, and that is collected and distributed by the state (Ross 2004). Indeed, weak states may create in a way their own demise, creating an opportunity structure for insurgent groups to form and mobilize, and control territory and wield authority outside of formal, legal frameworks (Fearon and Laitin 2003). Pakistan, for example, has seen local warlords and Islamist-inspired factions take control of vast swaths of its Western borderlands in the autonomous tribal regions, and at least one layer in its fragility is the conflict that has occurred when the state confronts these networks or attempts to use them in pursuit of its trans-border agenda in the fractious and volatile Southwest Asian region. Likewise, fragility in Nigeria is often seen as a consequence of the country's oil dependency, its distribution of rents through the state, and the volatile mix of ethnic and religious traditions (Umar 2007).

These social dimensions of vulnerability reflect a concern with the structure of society and the ways in which imbalances, discrimination, or the relationship between groups, economic opportunity, and states interact. Leading theories today associate the overlap between social class deprivation and identity as a critical and enduring cause of conflict. The expropriation of the symbols, power, and resources of the state to the exclusion of significant components of the population in multiethnic societies is a strong indicator of the likelihood of ethnic violence (Kaufman 2001). In these instances, group membership is an entitlement system of state-sanctioned status and wealth to the exclusion of others. Thus, ethnic fragmentation alone is not a condition that reflects vulnerability to conflict, rather, inter-group relations based on a history of prior ethnic enmity and ethnic discrimination or marginalization. The consequence is the often futile attempt by minority groups to secede or claim autonomy from existing states, such as the independence claims of Turkish Cypriots, the Kurdish separatist movement in Turkey, or the goal of some Kashmiri groups to become independent from both Pakistan and India.[16] When these self-determination claims clash against counter-claims by states of "territorial integrity," the seeds of conflict are often sown (Chesterman et al. 2001).

Several scholars have evaluated the importance of underlying demographic factors on conflict vulnerability, particularly those societies experiencing a "youth bulge" or large numbers of young people relative to the overall population (Cincotta et al. 2003; Cincotta 2009). As well, some social instability may arise from rapid urbanization in which deprivation in and around burgeoning developing world cities may create conditions of human insecurity in the absence of adequate, affordable housing.[17]

Denial of essential human needs is a critical, micro-level category of vulnerability. Countries at the very bottom of the global rankings on human development are also those that tend to be conflict-affected countries; thus, there is a hypothesized vicious cycle between chronic poverty and conflict. For example, conflict-affected countries are the site of today's most severe food security crises (Alinova et al. 2007). Typically, measures of essential human needs and of human development (such as the UNDP Human Development Index) indicate vulnerability to conflict, particularly in components of these indices that are closely associated with serious human suffering, for example infant or child mortality.

I. William Zartman persuasively argues that any single-factor or single-discipline theory of civil war is "profoundly uninteresting;" instead, interactions among these drivers at the intersection of "need, creed, and greed" should inform our understanding of the underlying causal relationships (2005: 257). This finding that conflict and fragility's root causes cannot be viewed in reductionist terms – i.e., "ethnic conflict" or "elite predation of lootable goods" – informs many of the complex, multiple-variable, multidimensional practitioner-oriented assessment frameworks that international organizations, governments, foreign direct investors, and donor organizations use to systematically assess conflict vulnerability within fragile states. These analytical instruments or toolkits seek to translate theories and concepts of deep drivers of civil war and post-war fragility into measurable indicators and causal pathways that lead to conflict escalation, often including an analysis of the state's capacity to cope with such pressures.[18]

After War: Fragile States

Civil war has devastating and long-lasting human and economic effects. In today's wars, civilians are targeted directly as the historically defined line between military combatants and civilians has been distinctly blurred (Chesterman 2001). One way to assess the human costs of war, beyond fatalities, is to consider the exponential increase in internal displacement and cross-border refugees that wars generate. In early 2000, at the height of the crisis of aftermath emanating from the wars of the 1990s, there were an estimated 21.5 million refugees and internally displaced persons; the vast number of these refugees and displaced were homeless from armed conflicts. Today, that number is similarly high, with the UN High Commissioner for Refugees (UNHCR) reporting that in 2011 there were 25.9 million refugees and internally displaced persons worldwide, with the top three countries hosting refugees all clearly within the "fragile" category themselves (Pakistan, DRC, and Kenya).[19]

Violent conflict also deeply affects economic performance and individual livelihoods and in the worst instances can precipitate "development in reverse" for countries as a whole, or reversals in prior levels of development as measured by indicators such as life expectancy or infant mortality (Hoeffler and Reynal-Querol 2003). At least one reason for the poor development outcomes in fragile states is the deep and long-lasting effects of conflict on health systems and the provision of basic services such as maternal and child care (Ghobarah et al. 2003).

Armed conflict also tends to metamorphose into other types of violence, particularly criminal violence. Even in contexts where peace agreements have ended the war and started a path to recovery, the root causes of armed conflict may not have been comprehensively addressed at the peace table; indeed, Achim Wennman has shown that economic factors are often central to peacemaking processes, yet the stakeholders in them may be unable or unwilling to address the structural conditions that give rise to violence (Wennman 2011). Social and economic stress, accompanied by political tensions and weak governance capacity, leave post-war countries highly vulnerable to renewed or new outbreaks of violence. Often, too, new social tensions emerge in post-war contexts, such as increased criminality, parallel economies, youth violence, and gender-based and sexual violence (Kurtenbach 2008). Countries such as South Africa, Guatemala, and Liberia have seen upsurges in crime in post-conflict environments, including gender-based violence in the immediate post-war period.

Violence can also emerge along ethnic or sectarian lines: the UN's Common Country Assessment (CCA) in Iraq in 2009 described succinctly the realities of fragility in Iraq after the externally induced collapse of the longstanding regime of former dictator Saddam Hussein following the US-led invasion in 2003. The 2009 UN report observed that:

> Iraq has made visible security and political progress since the peak of the post-2003 conflict. Violence has diminished considerably, particularly inter-sectarian conflict. Confidence in the state and a basic level of social trust are returning – albeit slowly in many areas. Still, the consequences of nearly three decades of detrimental economic and social policies, added

to the burden of war and violence, are becoming ever more apparent as the real work of governance begins.[20]

Fragility is felt directly by the people whose basic needs for security and human development are compromised by violence and pervasive personal insecurity. For example, in Iraq food insecurity has been one direct and common consequence of conflict and a lack of post-war development, particularly in areas where productive agricultural land is a prize over which the conflict is fought. The malicious policies of the Saddam Hussein regime in draining the delta-area marshlands of southern Iraq, affecting the mostly Shi'a community there (sometimes known as the "Marsh Arabs") destroyed their traditional patterns of livelihoods and threatened food security in these communities. In 2009, the UN Food and Agriculture Organization (FAO) began a major effort to restore the marshlands to address the linkage between the livelihoods of those in the areas destroyed by Hussein's government and the restoration of the marshland ecosystem as a way to recreate the resilience of these communities in the face of threats to food security.[21]

In Liberia, too, the effect of the war on state capacity to enable development was pervasive: the security forces under Taylor became a "state within a state," government ministries either collapsed or became mechanisms for rent-seeking and banal graft, service delivery collapsed, especially in ungovernable rebel-held areas, and the country's financial institutions failed to function. During the Liberian civil war (1989–96, and again from 1999 to 2003), there was also a deep human security crisis, with widespread recruitment of child soldiers, deployment of landmines, and proliferation of small arms, an eviscerated economic and social infrastructure, and among the lowest human development indicators in the world. In human terms, as a consequence of conflict, large segments of the population – especially the educated professionals – simply fled the country.[22]

As for the Liberian state, the government led by Charles Taylor was disincentivized to rebuild formal state institutions that had been destroyed during the first Liberian civil war (1989–1996), and those remaining – such as the armed forces – were emaciated in order to forward the interests of a select, elite group (Gberie 2007: 210). Without functioning governance, and in the face of acute human security threats, development plummeted and the deprivation that ensued continues to be the principal source of challenges to peacebuilding.[23] In terms of gross domestic product (GDP) per capita, Liberia ranked 169 out of 181 countries in 2009.[24]

In post-war transitional periods, rapid political change, economic crises, external shocks from the global or regional context, and troubled electoral processes have been identified as risks to the sustainability of peace (Collier et al. 2008). Countries emerging from conflict do seem predisposed to violence in the early phases of the transition: political crises threaten delicate peacebuilding processes and these crises often generate reversals in progress toward the consolidation of peace (Höglund 2008). This is true despite well-intentioned efforts to chart out what progress in statebuilding actually means, and to develop indicators on increasing the authority, capacity, or legitimacy of the state (see, e.g., Cohen 2006). Instability of the constitutional framework (uncertainty as to the rules of the game) and governing coalitions raise the political volatility in turbulent transitions from war to peace and often precipitate violent clashes. Such political crises, particularly electoral moments or long periods of incoherent transitional regimes, can serve as conflict triggers or accelerators of underlying conditions such as ethnic difference (Snyder 2000).

Critically, state weakness is seen as a key factor in the continued vulnerability of countries to repeated crisis and disruptive shocks: without a viable system of governance to mediate disputes and reconcile social interests, grievances and frustrations quickly find outlets through organized violence (Fearon and Laitin 2004). Some suggest that developing world countries feature social and economic structures that incentivize predatory or corrupt elite behavior.[25]

Beyond the impact of chronic fragility on human resources or the functioning of specific institutions, conflicts fracture social relationships, diminishing the collective capacity of societies to recover. And where there are social tensions and elite opportunities combined with scarcity, inter-communal tensions can erupt, often over resources or economic opportunities of advantaged or disadvantaged groups (Horowitz 2001). In the aftermath of civil war and in the midst of uncertain transitions, a general sense of mistrust and suspicion toward the state and emerging leadership groups commonly prevails. In turn, underlying political, social, economic, and environmental stressors cannot be managed by capable local sources of authority. Thus, there is a vicious cycle of violence, state weakness, social dislocation, and economic and environmental deterioration in most countries that suffer from the fragility syndrome.

After civil war, fledging regimes face enormous legitimacy challenges. New post-war regimes led by erstwhile insurgents must gain trust from the people to become recognized as leaders and legitimate in their exercise of power and authority. For example, in Nepal following the Comprehensive Peace Agreement and Interim Constitution of 2007, an ongoing challenge has been the reintegration of former rebel challengers into government and forming a stable coalition among the country's more than 20 political parties. The question of inclusion is often paired with the need for transforming the political economy of social arrangements, in that political inclusion also brings platforms of socio-economic change aimed at redressing the overlap between identity and socio-economic disadvantage. In the post-war contexts, traditional leaders and customary law institutions have an important role to play in peacebuilding and service delivery, and often these informal institutions that served society through the war, such as traditional justice systems, can have more legitimacy than any formal government.

Assessing and Measuring Fragility

The multidimensional nature of the fragility syndrome – which is both state-based and society-based – suggests the need to develop more valid and reliable measures of vulnerability to violence at both structural and precipitant-event levels of analysis. In response to this challenge, some good, quantitatively based, large comparative research projects have sought to measure fragility. Research on the underlying vulnerabilities tends to isolate the central factors of social, economic, and political conditions that are common in countries affected by armed conflict and armed violence (Marshall and Cole 2011).

Governance matters: indeed, it is the axis around which the vulnerabilities to conflict interact with the official and unofficial institutions and processes through which social conflict is putatively managed. The type of regime is seen as a critical factor: the more repressive a regime, for example in authoritarian settings, the greater the likelihood that it will engage in conflict internally (for purposes of repression) or in conflict with democratic states (Hermann and Kegley 2001). Thus, assessments of vulnerability to conflict should also include a close look at variables such as the level of militarization and repression by a state. Critical in this regard is the analysis of the human rights record of a state and, in particular, violations of human rights as measured in some indices such as those that assess levels of extrajudicial killings.

Criminality, lawlessness, and threats of armed violence are also closely related to conflict vulnerability, and indeed there is increasing interest in evaluating the interaction among social violence, vulnerability to armed conflict, and actual occurrence of armed violence.[26] This interest has equally been influential in including in the statebuilding discourse the need for strategic approaches to armed violence reduction (Muggah and Krause 2009).

In sum, analytical approaches to fragility tend to focus on four sets of critical factors:

- The first is *social aspects* of vulnerability, such as demographic instabilities in which there are large numbers of underemployed, and often undereducated, youth;
- *Economic vulnerabilities*, such as high rates of chronic poverty, or exposure to primary commodity price fluctuations,
- *Governance variables*, such as the effectiveness of public administration in delivering public goods; and
- *Security*, especially the presence or absence of large-scale violence (including interpersonal, inter-communal, or civil war).

In a recent study, six major research projects of fragility were systematically compared for their ability to capture and measure the fragility concept; this study found that most of these measures produced similar results in terms of the countries on the globe deemed to be most fragile or failed by various empirical research projects (Hughes et al. 2011).[27] Comparative research and large-scale quantitative approaches like the study cited above yield some interesting findings. There is increasing consensus on what constitutes "vulnerability to violence," and there is increasingly good tracking of countries globally to measure these structural conditions. These systematic approaches to measuring fragility also allow for greater understanding of the structural determinants of violence to be paired with in-depth knowledge of a country to produce a blended understanding of the nature of the state-building challenge in any particular case.

Although all of these research projects have their merits, and they find similar results in any event, in my view the very best source for up-to-date measurement of all states in the international system on these variables is found in the work of the Center for Systemic Peace, reflected in its most recent *Global Report 2011: Conflict, Governance, and State Fragility* (Marshall and Cole 2011).[28] This report ranked the most fragile states in the international system, and presented here are the top three categories of most-fragile countries based on this report's specific methodology, and they provide a starting point for discussion about which states in the world are most fragile. In table 1.1, I have also coded those countries that have seen civil war or extensive political violence in recent years as a way to highlight the close linkages between fragility and vulnerability to such violence. Table 1.2 presents one of the summary findings of the meta-analysis of quantitative measures of fragility mentioned above (Hughes et al. 2011); as suggested above, we found a very high degree of inter-correlation among the various research projects and some consensus on which states have essentially failed (Rotberg 2003), which are highly fragile, those that are vulnerable, and those that were measured as mostly stable and where peace is mostly consolidated. The fact that Syria, which slipped into civil war in 2011, did not make the top rankings in table 1.1 is indicative of the fact that some putatively stable countries can experience "punctuated equilibrium," as Stephen Krasner has argued (1984), such that narrow, corrupt, or exclusive autocratic regimes may well be more vulnerable to violence than they appear on the surface.

Table 1.1 Most Fragile States, 2011	
1.	Somalia*
2.	Sudan (includes South Sudan)*
3.	Democratic Republic of Congo*
4.	Afghanistan*
5.	Chad*
6.	Myanmar (Burma)*
7.	Ethiopia*
8.	Côte d'Ivoire*
9.	Sierra Leone*
10.	Burundi*
11.	Central African Republic*
12.	Guinea*
13.	Haiti*
14.	Liberia*
15.	Niger*
16.	Burkina Faso
17.	Guinea-Bissau*
18.	Iraq*
19.	Nigeria*
20.	Rwanda*
21.	Uganda*
22.	Zimbabwe*
23.	Angola*
24.	Cameroon
25.	Congo-Brazzaville*
26.	Malawi
27.	Mauritania
28.	Yemen*
29.	Algeria*
30.	Gambia
31.	Nepal*
32.	Pakistan*

Table 1.1	(continued)
33.	Zambia
34.	Ghana
35.	Kyrgyzstan*
36.	Madagascar
37.	Mali*
38.	Mozambique*
39.	Comoros*
40.	Djibouti
41.	Egypt*
42.	Laos
43.	Sri Lanka*
44.	Timor Leste*
45.	Togo*
46.	Uzbekistan
47.	Bangladesh*
48.	Benin
49.	Cambodia*
50.	Colombia*
51.	Ecuador
52.	Eritrea*
53.	Iran*
54.	Kenya*
55.	Tajikistan*
56.	Tanzania

* Civil war or significant episodes of political violence (coded by the author).
Source: Marshall and Cole (2011: 30–2)

Table 1.2: Combined Assessment of Fragility from Six Quantitative Studies

Spectrum Analysis Cohort Members (2011)

Failing 3	Fragile 48	Vulnerable 72	Stable 59
Afghanistan	Algeria	Albania	Argentina
Congo, Democratic Republic of	Angola	Armenia	Australia
Somalia	Bangladesh	Azerbaijan	Austria
	Burkina Faso	Belarus	Bahamas, The
	Burundi	Belize	Bahrain
	Cambodia	Benin	Barbados
	Cameroon	Bhutan	Belgium
	Central African Republic	Bolivia	Botswana
	Chad	Bosnia and Herzegovina	Brunei
	Comoros	Brazil	Bulgaria
	Congo, Republic of	Cape Verde	Canada
	Cote d'Ivoire	China	Chile
	Djibouti	Colombia	Costa Rica
	Equatorial Guinea	Cuba	Croatia
	Eritrea	Dominican Republic	Cyprus
	Ethiopia	Ecuador	Czech Republic
	Gambia, The	Egypt, Arab Republic of	Denmark
	Guinea	El Salvador	Estonia
	Guinea-Bissau	Fiji	Finland
	Haiti	Gabon	France
	Iran, Islamic Republic of	Georgia	Germany
	Iraq	Ghana	Greece
	Kenya	Guatemala	Grenada

Table 1.2: (continued)

Spectrum Analysis Cohort Members (2011)

Failing 3	Fragile 48	Vulnerable 72	Stable 59
	Korea, Democratic People's Republic of	Guyana	Hong Kong
	Laos, People's Democratic Republic	Honduras	Hungary
	Liberia	India	Iceland
	Malawi	Indonesia	Ireland
	Mauritania	Israel	Italy
	Mozambique	Jamaica	Japan
	Myanmar	Jordan	Korea, Republic of
	Nepal	Kazakhstan	Kuwait
	Niger	Kyrgyz Republic	Latvia
	Nigeria	Lebanon	Lithuania
	Pakistan	Lesotho	Luxembourg
	Palestine	Libya	Malaysia
	Rwanda	Macedonia, Former Yugoslav Republic of	Malta
	Sierra Leone	Madagascar	Mauritius
	Sri Lanka	Maldives	Montenegro
	Sudan	Mali	Netherlands
	Swaziland	Mexico	New Zealand
	Tajikistan	Micronesia, Fed. Sts.	Norway
	Timor-Leste	Moldova	Oman
	Togo	Mongolia	Panama
	Uganda	Morocco	Poland
	Uzbekistan	Namibia	Portugal

Table 1.2: (continued)

Spectrum Analysis Cohort Members (2011)

Failing 3	Fragile 48	Vulnerable 72	Stable 59
	Yemen, Republic of	Nicaragua	Romania
	Zambia	Papua New Guinea	Samoa
	Zimbabwe	Paraguay	Singapore
		Peru	Slovak Republic
		Philippines	Slovenia
		Qatar	Spain
		Russian Federation	St. Lucia
		Sao Tome and Principe	Sweden
		Saudi Arabia	Switzerland
		Senegal	Taiwan, China
		Serbia	United Arab Emirates
		Solomon Islands	United Kingdom
		South Africa	United States
		St. Vincent and the Grenadines	Uruguay
		Suriname	
		Syrian Arab Republic	
		Tanzania	
		Thailand	
		Tonga	
		Trinidad and Tobago	
		Tunisia	
		Turkey	
		Turkmenistan	

Table 1.2: (continued)			
Spectrum Analysis Cohort Members (2011)			
Failing 3	*Fragile 48*	*Vulnerable 72*	*Stable 59*
		Ukraine	
		Vanuatu	
		Venezuela	
		Vietnam	

Source: Hughes et al. (2011: 72)

Conclusion

The concept and language of fragility found in contemporary scholarly and policy circles describe well the problems that civil war leaves in its wake. At the same time, comparative research on countries labeled "fragile" has shown that progress toward the 2000–15 global development targets, or Millennium Development Goals (MDGs), in the fragile states is in fact rather uneven and that the fragility concept may not capture well the varieties of situations that confront twenty-first-century statebuilding (Harttgen and Klasen 2010). Thus, there is caution in terms of its precision as a concept, and care should be exercised in its usage. Politically, too, no government wants to be labeled as "fragile" – and especially not "failed" – and in recent high-level policy documents, there is usage of the rather glossed-over term "states experiencing conflict and fragility."[29] Yet ultimately, the fragility concept has emerged as the best, perhaps least common denominator approach to evaluating the challenges that the statebuilding approach seeks to address. Indeed, "fragility" has more or less replaced the earlier nomenclature of "failed" states that captured the collapse of Somalia in the late 1980s or the relatively rapid implosion of the Qadhafi regime in 2011.

Ultimately, as the listing in table 1.1 suggests, fragility is perhaps best characterized as a spectrum, with on the one hand situations where the state is weakened so as to be wholly incapacitated or shattered, as in Somalia, or where new states are created anew (as in Timor-Leste), to situations in which there is a relatively strong state in the wake of civil war, but conflict has either limited its legitimacy and authority in key regions or among sections of the population (as in Sri Lanka or Uganda). Thus, the fragility concept is further defined in the context of varieties of starting points for statebuilding which are developed more fully in chapter 3. For now, without a better alternative concept and discourse, the "fragility" nomenclature is widely accepted as the way to describe the woe of aftermath following today's civil wars. The extent, drivers, and consequences of fragility are in fact the starting point in the statebuilding debate in the transition from conflict to consolidation.[30]

Before evaluating today's statebuilding debates, however, it is salutary to revisit some core theories and understandings of the state, and to understand how the role and purposes of the state have evolved – and broadened – into the twenty-first century.

CHAPTER TWO

The State into the Twenty-first Century

Today's notion of statebuilding – emphasizing the interplay between international assistance and domestic processes – has conceptual antecedents in the long evolution of the contemporary international system which is based on the state as its core foundation. The historical dynamics of the past inform the present through a look back at how modern statebuilding occurred initially in Western Europe,[1] and later in post-colonial states in which Europeans drew many boundaries and created entities of authority that are now taken more or less for granted. What ties historical and new theories of statebuilding together is the common analysis on the state in terms of its autonomy (or freedom from foreign influence or capture by narrow domestic interests), authority (as the sole, legitimate use of coercive force), capacity (the state's ability to formulate and deliver governance services), and its legitimacy (its internal and external "right" to rule). This conceptual framework serves as the basis for this book, recognizing of course that these concepts are often related and at times mutually interdependent: the state's authority, or ability to rule, for example, is often a function of its legitimacy, or the right to rule based on consent of the governed.

Building a state is really about expanding the ability of governing elites and public administrators (to include, for example, the military and police as well as local elected officials and civil servants) to formulate a set of visions and goals for society and to achieve them through collective action for social progress (for example, the reduction of infant mortality rates) and for economic gain (for example, achieving greater rates of employment). Many studies in comparative politics have pondered the nature of the state, how contemporary states were formed, and whether the state is an autonomous political actor or whether it is simply reflective of dominant social forces.

Some theorists consider the state as principally a reflection of social forces within societies that claim a common destiny as a nation, and thus any concept of the state must be grounded in the dominant economic and social relationships within a political community. Karl Marx and Friedrich Engels, for example, famously commented that "the executive of the modern state is nothing but a committee for managing the common affairs of the whole bourgeoisie," arguing that the structure of class relations (particularly in nineteenth-century Europe) meant that the state served the interests of the ruling class (Marx and Engels 2006).[2] The state as a tool of social forces was seen by Vladimir Lenin, especially, as the strategic asset of the revolutionary vanguard of the proletariat; Lenin, in his 1917 tract *State and Revolution*, calls for the revolutionary elite to "smash" the ancient, feudal Czarist state in order for vanguard elites to recreate it to serve the goals of the socialist revolution (Lenin 2009 [1918]).[3]

Classic works in theories of the state typically depart from the work of Max Weber, the nineteenth- and early twentieth-century German sociologist who studied the increasing rationalization (in terms of bureaucratic rationality, i.e., the rise of a neutral civil "service") and secularization of the state. Weber argued against Karl Marx's conceptualization of the state as reflecting the dominance of capitalist classes (until after the communist revolution, that is, after which Marx argued the state would wither away as unnecessary), suggesting that we should view the historical evolution of the state as a process of moving away from forms of charismatic domination (family or religious grounds for rule, such as the lineage of royalty and the divine right of kings), and traditional domination (by patriarchs, patrimonial systems of lord and subject, or feudal relationships), toward what he described as "legal domination," in which society is governed by modern law and a state with its professional bureaucracy and its commitment to evidence-based or knowledge-oriented rule (Mommsen 1992: 46). Weber's seminal work on this topic is his 1922 essay *Economy and Society*, which appeared after his death from the Spanish flu at the early age of 56; in this essay he lays out many of the core ideas of rational-legal approaches to authority and to public administration that continue to inform global approaches to statebuilding today (Weber 1968 [1922]).

State Formation and the Contemporary State System

The debate on the nature of the state in relation to social forces is informed by a critical question: How did the international state system emerge in the first place – that is, what do we know about the process of state formation – and how were "states" built in the past? Can there be inferences from the essentially internal – and often bloody – prior experiences in statebuilding that inform contemporary approaches? The modern state system has its origins in the evolution in Western Europe from the models of centralization of authority under absolute monarchs; states emerged, historically, in part from the battles and struggles of kings to protect themselves from external threats, to rule over feudal lords who might challenge their supremacy, to extend authority over often autonomous city-states, and to curb the power of religious authorities over society (Tilly 1975, 1990). Charles Tilly famously penned that "War made the state and the state made war" (1975: 42). In contrast, others contend that the origins of the European state are found in the underlying growth of trade and the demands of merchant classes for security and clarity in governance rules, particularly protection from extraneous taxation (Spruyt 2009: 216–17).

Successful statebuilding depended significantly on resource extraction: the ability of powerful monarchs to accumulate revenue through taxes, conquest and exploits, and, over time, the provision of services by bureaucratic authorities to address popular demands (Tilly 1985). In post-medieval Europe, the Spanish and Austro-Hungarian empires emerged as predecessors to what appears like modern states, in which the authorities become directly associated with fixed borders and territories, and eventually the European empires of Spain, Portugal, Holland, Sweden, France, and England began to extend this control of territory to far-flung colonies, based in large part on the desire for accumulation of resources and an extraction-from-society approach. For this reason, in part, Mancur Olson developed the notion of the state as a "stationary bandit," reflecting his view that the state is no more than the sum total of rational individuals who seek positions in the state in pursuit of their own self-interest and work together – much like an organized criminal group – to use extractive methods for their own advancement (Olson 2000: 3–24).

The Peace of Westphalia in 1648, which ended the Thirty Years War of internecine religious struggles brought on by the Reformation, is typically seen as the date of the dawn of the modern state system. The principles of mutual rights and obligations of states to each other are found in the series of agreements among European powers of the age to divide territory and to mutually recognize each other's sovereign authority. Although today it is common to think of the states in Western Europe as reflecting a natural division of national groups (in general), today's states emerged through aggregation, war, and conquest, and often their own internal revolutions and civil wars to get to the point of the establishment of state authority that is seen today. Germany and Italy were only unified in 1871 following the Franco-Prussian war.

The enshrinement of the state concept in international law, in which the notion of sovereignty is codified, is reflected in the Montevideo Convention of 1933, which offers the only precise definition of a state in codified international law: a permanent population, a specified territory, a government, and the capacity to enter into relations with other states.[4] Whether any claimant to become a state can be judged as worthy depends much on international recognition of the state, which, once granted, has never been revoked even in cases like Somalia where, in the midst of anarchy, outsiders could not find externally or internally legitimate custodians of the state (Herbst 2000).[5] Thus, the concept of the state is very much the product of constructed realities over the years, and while states have legal personhood in the international system, the realities of states in today's fragile context may reflect the lack of consensus on who legitimately governs.

In China, the history of statebuilding has been about the concentration of authority of the central state against the historically powerful warlords who controlled, initially, water rights and irrigation (Wittfogel 1981) and, in more recent periods, the prevailing of a central state over warlords who had captured the opium trade (Zhou 1999). Suisheng Zhao (2004) has shown how the modern Chinese Communist Party has furthered the process of statebuilding by constructing a vision of Chinese nationalism that is reactive to a history of foreign occupation and a shared sense of humiliation and that has evolved from a universalistic empire into a modern socially constructed nation-state.

Ultimately, modern states and the national identities they reflect are very much "imagined communities," in the ringing words of Benedict Anderson (1991). And, once in power, elites with statebuilding aspirations have a tendency to "invent mass-producing traditions," among them rituals of power and authority, monuments and grand capitals, and events such as public holidays, to further legitimate and perpetuate mass loyalty to the nation and to the state (Hobsbawn 1983). To the extent that the identity of a state is tied to the construction of the idea of a "nation," it is perhaps useful to recall George Orwell's definition of "nationalism," penned just after the devastation of World War II in 1945, as "the lunatic modern habit of identifying oneself with large power units and seeing everything in terms of competitive prestige" (1968 [1945]: 43).

In many states, colonization and empire had the effect of disseminating through international conquest the boundaries and borders of the contemporary state system. State formation at the end of the colonial era meant that state personhood was inherited, not constructed internally (Vu 2010); for example, the creation of modern Pakistan and India occurred as a consequence of the partition of British colonial India in 1948. In the course of creating these new states, whether in South Asia or in post-colonial Africa (where independent leaders agreed not to revisit colonial-era boundaries), older informal authorities were often left intact as colonial leaders worked through these institutions rather than replacing them (for example, the Mogul Empire in India). Often colonial states were not service providers, but exploitative oppressors that used local proxies to extract rent and resources from subservient populations. In these post-colonial situations, state formation has been driven by internal forces and by external dynamics, particularly, as Charles Tilly points out, by the three factors of colonial possession, governance structures determined by colonialism, and by the politics of external recognition (1990).

Many leaders of independence movements, communist and non-communist among them, have adopted Lenin's view of the state as a tool for a missionary transformation of society; more often than not, these grand projects have failed (Scott 1999). In post-colonial settings, the great historical state-building projects of charismatic leaders such as Mohandas Gandhi in India, Kwame Nkrumah in Ghana, or Abdel Nasser in Egypt reflected a vision to use the power of the state and the legitimacy of the anti-colonialism struggle to transform society to create a new nationalism to accompany statehood as such. Where successful, such as in Tanzania under Julius Nyerere, nation building in post-colonial settings is often seen in terms of exceptionalism (Green 2011) in contrast to the realities of contested claims between state and nation that has afflicted many other Africa countries (Larémont 2005). As eminent scholar Juan Linz has argued, "The difficulties of making every nation a state and every state a nation, and the fact that people live intermingled within the borders of states and have different and often dual identity leads to arguments for multi-national states, states which abandon the dream of becoming nation states and 'nations' willing to live in a multi-national democratic liberal state" (Linz 1993: 355).

Given these historical processes, today's states emerged mostly throughout the twentieth century as the building blocks of the contemporary state system; at the founding of the United Nations in 1945 in San Francisco, there were 51 original member states in the contemporary international system. Today's states, now numbering 193 with the independence of South Sudan in 2011 following decades of civil war, have legal sovereignty internationally and seek domestic legitimacy internally as their primary characteristic (Krasner 1984).

Today, Kosovo and Palestine are waiting in the wings to eventually have their sovereignty universally recognized. Although many states have been recognized in the wake of internal war, such as Bangladesh, Eritrea, or Timor-Leste, which emerged following the end of civil wars, in these instances there was typically reference to antecedents of colonialism and the mistakes of decolonization that justified international recognition. The recognition of South Sudan in 2011, together with the proposed independence and recognition by many states of Kosovo in terms of the Ahtisaari Plan,[6] portends a new era in which it may be possible for new states to emerge. Still, these new countries in the making are still exceptions in what is a strong bias internationally against the partition of existing states even when the boundaries of the state do not coincide with citizen perceptions of what constitutes the "nation" (Sambanis 2000).

Autonomy, Authority, Capacity, and Legitimacy

As the history of state formation has evolved, so, too, have social-science theories of the state in terms of its purpose, structures, and functions. During the so-called behavioralist revolution of the post-World War II era, scholars in a society-centered perspective tended to see the state not in terms of an autonomous actor, but (a bit like Marx, but in a different way) as reflective of social forces. Political scientists such as David Easton (1965) argued that the state is more of a system, and that one should think more in terms of "government" than in terms of the state as something bigger than the sum of its parts (people, buildings, resources, etc.). Systems theorists were more interested in evaluating the social inputs into the politics (political behavior that creates demands or supports for action by the state) and outputs, or decisions that lead to a particular action. Easton and others considered systems of governance that are stable and those that are dysfunctional as a way to differentiate when government did, or did not, work.

Because the systems theory perspective does not explain well how social inputs translate into policy outputs (the problem of the state as a "black box"), influential scholars such as Theda Skocpol and others argued for "bringing the state back in" to analysis as an *autonomous* actor. Skocpol's seminal state-centered perspective on the state defines it in collective and structural terms, arguing that the state itself has some *autonomy* from social forces. State officials, for example, are indeed strong agents of action to shape society; Skocpol defines the state as

> a set of administrative, policing and military organizations headed, and more or less well coordinated by, an executive authority. Any state first and fundamentally extracts resources from society and deploys these to create and support coercive and administrative organizations (1985: 29).

That is, the state cannot be reduced to the incentives and interests of the people who lead or work in government, but that the state has autonomy and endurance as an actor in its own right. Politicians and bureaucrats may come and go, but the state endures and persists. As we shall see in the next chapter, the notion of autonomy today can also be interpreted as the state's ability to be free from foreign intervention and external influence, including custodial control by ostensibly well-meaning international peacebuilders in what some astute observers have termed "neo-trusteeship" (Fearon and Laitin 2004; Zaum 2007).

In addition to autonomy, the second characteristic of the state is *authority*. Weber argued famously that the state "claims the monopoly of legitimate force in a given territory" (Weber 1921). How this monopoly is claimed, however, has been in part through wars of conquest, civil strife, and often bloody struggles for power. Anthony Giddens (1985) has argued that the process of statebuilding is about the removal of violence from politics, and in the process of regulation of the state's use of violence through police (internally) and the military (in theory, externally) by the rule of law and associated administrative processes. He argues that modern states emerged from mutually reinforcing dynamics of political processes, such as external war and inter-state conflict, and through economic processes of capitalism and industrial development.

Tilly (1975, 1985, 1990) shows that state formation[7] and statebuilding have emerged historically largely out of external and internal war-making, through which states seek to expand and to secure external stability; through internal war, in which leaders emerge victorious over internal rivals; and through the political economy of taxation and the ability to raise recurring sources of revenue in order to fund the war and to protect allies. As is described in chapter 3, contemporary statebuilding efforts are first and foremost focused on establishing or re-establishing the authority of the state.

Joel Migdal (1988) describes the state-making pathway as an essentially sequential process. In the first phase, the aspirant sovereign uses coercion to define the boundaries of the "nation." Challenges to authority are violently suppressed, and competing claims of sovereignty are quashed, and the state as such prevails over informal institutions like the Church. In the second phase, the state's subjects begin to comply: they accept taxation, and they individually and collectively yield to the supreme authority of the "state" as law. Over time, historically, citizens begin self-identifying with the state as citizens and they begin to perceive the state as a "good" institution. Migdal sums up the history of statebuilding in these striking terms: "The strength of the state organization in an environment of conflict has depended in large part on the social control it has exercised" (1988: 33). That is, the *capacity* of the state is not a matter of how many weapons it may have, or its ability to coerce citizens through taxation, but rather on the consent and relationship of the state to its society and its consent to be governed.

This focus on state authority and its capacity to formulate and implement a national vision and specific policy objectives is augmented by the fourth consideration, that of *legitimacy*. For this reason, theories of the state have moved further from "bringing the state back in" to understanding the "state-in-society" as a useful lens through which to evaluate statebuilding processes (Migdal et al. 1994; Migdal 2001). From this perspective, we see that under charismatic or transformational leaders, states may seek to shape their societies through grand social projects and that, in turn, societies can shape the nature and capacity of the state through the extent or absence of social cohesion. Migdal calls for a view to see the state in terms of "reinforcing and contradictory practices and alliances of its disparate parts" (2001: 22). Contemporary theories of the state thus see the state as embedded in, and often shaped by, its society; state–society relations emerged as an approach to the state in the 1980s to reflect the importance of the mutual influences that states have on their societies, and vice versa, and this approach informs the evolution of the concept into its contemporary uses in international security and development policy.

Ultimately, the notion that the state is the sole custodian of coercion in society – often reflected most poignantly to citizens in the form of the policeman's badge – is central to the idea of the state. But authority, like capacity, cannot be wielded if it is considered illegitimate by the citizens. That is, in the absence of a social contract, the state's authority is but a thin reed of coercive power, and the capacity of the state to implement its visions and policies will be, ultimately, ineffective.[8] States today require both external legitimacy – recognition of their sovereignty by outside authority, principally membership of the United Nations – and internal legitimacy, or embeddedness in their societies. Peter Evans, for example, has argued that the autonomous power of the state to get things done derives from the extent to which it is deeply supported by various social groups in pursuit of a very specific view of economic development (1995). That is, legitimacy comes not just from being the guardian of the nation from external harm, or perhaps from claiming a religious basis of legitimacy (as in contemporary Iran), but from its development performance.

There is much debate today about the various elements and aspects of state legitimacy in terms of state–society relations. Legitimacy, like the concept of quality, is highly subjective and defies a precise definition. A study for the OECD-DAC reaffirmed that traditional approaches to thinking about state legitimacy require rethinking for contemporary, post-war environments. The authors contend that:

> [The] formal institutions of the Western state derive their capacity and legitimacy from a long history of interaction between state and society, and [this concept] cannot be reproduced simply by transferring the same institutional models into different social and political contexts (OECD-DAC 2010b: 7).

Instead, we must think about the legitimacy of the contemporary state – especially in the immediate aftermath of civil war – as complex, multifaceted, and multidimensional and derived from a variety of external and internal sources. As reflected in the chapters that follow, and especially chapter 6, legitimacy today is intricately linked with and related to the dimensions of autonomy, authority, and capacity. Legitimacy of states today does seem to come principally from international recognition, but also by the state's input or process legitimacy through which rulers are chosen or laws are made through agreed-upon rules or procedures; through output or performance legitimacy, of the ability to effectively provide public goods of security or the conditions for economic development; and through shared beliefs, or traditional sources such as a common national identity and beliefs shaped by

religion, tradition, or the personality-cult following of transformative leaders.

This expanded notion of legitimacy means that statebuilding is actually not just about empowering the state, but rather
the ability of state authorities and institutions to interact with
society – civic organizations, associations, and citizen groups
– and to work together in partnerships (including, in many
contexts today, international organizations), to achieve public
goods (Putnam et al. 1994). The Nobel prize-winning scholar
Elinor Ostrom has shown that the state institutions are most
effective at creating such public goods when they have worked
with civil society at various levels of organization (1996). This
theme of partnerships will be picked up in the final chapter,
which describes how interaction across a wide range of actors
– from the global to the local – is a strong characteristic of the
contemporary statebuilding regime in post-war countries. For
this reason, too, it is common to think today less about the role
of government as such, and more in terms of "governance" as
a way to include a look at both the formal institutions and processes of the state and the more informal rules of the same for
exercising power and implementing policies (Hyden 1999).

A Twenty-first-century State: Toward
Development and Democracy?

The International Commission on State Sovereignty (ICSS), a
high-level group of eminent persons brought together under
the authority of the Canadian government, was asked by
then-Secretary-General of the UN, Kofi Annan, to explore the
responsibility of states today to protect their citizens from dire
threats to their personal safety – and especially from atrocities, historically often committed by fearful, autocratic rulers
clinging to power – in operationalizing the new principle of
the Responsibility to Protect (R2P; see chapter 7). Indeed, the

Commission endorsed and defined the boundaries of the R2P concept that says that states must protect their citizens from harm, but they also went further to define a less well-known international "responsibility to rebuild." The Commission argued that:

> The responsibility to protect implies the responsibility not just to prevent and react but to follow through and rebuild. This means that if military intervention action is taken – because of a breakdown or abdication of a state's own capacity and authority in discharging its 'responsibility to protect' – there should be a genuine commitment to helping to build a durable peace, and promoting good governance and sustainable development. Conditions of public safety and order have to be reconstituted by international agents acting in partnership with local authorities, with the goal of progressively transferring to them authority and responsibility to rebuild (ICSS 2001: 39).

What kind of state should the international community commit to rebuilding? As states have emerged to exercise authority and to define the boundaries of the political community, the concomitant idea of states as the outcome of social contracts that go beyond the provision of security informs the conceptualization of the state today. Although service provision by states was often related to managing internal risks (such as disease outbreaks and the extension of public health services), as prosperity grew in Western states, there was the evolution of the concept of the state as a provider of essential services, particularly universal primary education (Hobsbawn 1983). Social contract approaches today emphasize not just security, or even service delivery, but also the state as the ultimate protector of human rights in society – including individual rights, but increasingly the rights of disadvantaged and vulnerable populations, including women, migrants, the disabled, and cultural and religious minorities.[9]

States today must be inclusive, both normatively in terms of international human rights and practically in terms of effective governance through broad participation of the poor and marginalized as a precursor to broader social stability (see chapter 1). For outsiders, this means helping fragile countries formulate national action plans to improve women's participation in post-war governance, and further the mainstreaming of women's representation and influence across the governance domain (i.e., within government and within civil society). United Nations Development Program (UNDP) projects, for example, have featured initiatives to enhance women's participation in post-war governance, efforts to redress and prevent sexual violence, support for public awareness campaigns on issues such as violence against women, assistance in the creation of women-oriented units in various government ministries, assistance to national human rights commissions to help mainstream gender issues into overall efforts to promote human rights protections, projects that address women's issues in the justice sector (e.g., criminal investigations or women's access to justice), and attention to gender issues in processes of state budgeting and allocation of resources (Castillejo 2011). The focus on gender underscores the fact that internationalized statebuilding today is guided not only by practical political, economic, and social issues, but also by the adoption and implementation of global norms of human rights that emerged following World War II and the very creation of the United Nations in its wake.[10]

Thus, any notion of the state (and of statebuilding) today must include not just its role in securing territory and establishing authority, but of a state committed to socio-economic development and to being the core provider of public goods such as water and sanitation, health care, critical infrastructures (such as telecommunication regulation), and education, and as the outcome of a social contract based on the legitimacy that flows from state–society relations. Such service delivery in turn requires a professional public administration, or one in which the civil service is based on merit and competence – not family, regional, party-political, or ethnic ties – and the norms through which a legal/rational bureaucracy owes its loyalty first to the state and its people and only in a subsidiary way to the elites who may govern it.

Conclusion

Statebuilding today has many of the same elements as historical processes of state formation and the expansion of autonomy, authority, capacity, and legitimacy. According to Ghani et al. (2006), states today perform at least ten core functions. They are to: exercise legitimate monopoly on the means of violence; exercise administrative control or make rules and regulations; manage public finances; invest in human capital; delineate citizenship rights and duties; provide infrastructure services; form and regulate markets; manage collective assets, including natural resources, cultural assets, and the environment; conduct international relations; and implement the rule of law.

Modern functions of the state equally include demands for the state to: prevent as far as possible future natural disasters or man-made disasters such as famine; develop adequate and accurate early-warning systems of impending disaster; protect the most vulnerable elements of society, such as poor workers, the disabled, the elderly or the diseased; promote economic growth that alleviates the plight of the world's extremely poor; and address the distribution of income and wealth in societies to ensure that the poor benefit through employment opportunities, higher wages, security of assets, and the ability to participate in the economy. With global norms such as the Convention on the Elimination of Discrimination against

Women (CEDAW), states that are signatories to this regime are also obligated to advance the equality of women, who as a global class are consistently seen in indicators of human development as less well-off in life choices than men. States are also required to: develop democratic institutions and processes that empower all segments of society to participate equitably in political, economic, and social life and that do not allow for social exclusion, intolerance, or bigotry; create conditions for environmental sustainability and the prevention of long-term ecological instabilities that will produce future economic catastrophes; and create opportunity for local action, direct citizen participation, and community-level problem-solving. These demands on the modern state are in sum a tall order, especially given what we know of fragile state contexts as highlighted in the previous chapter.

While states are still putatively sovereign (autonomous and independent), many of today's contemporary challenges – international and national security, economic development, environmental sustainability, and public health to name a few – cannot be managed by states acting alone. In a globalized world, today's transnational realities require re-conceptualization of the state and society in an era of "global governance" in which many challenges spill across borders (Simmons and Oudraat 2001).

Thus, I argue that there is a need to employ a distinctly twenty-first-century look at the changing and, indeed, expanding nature of an ideal state in an increasingly interdependent world, characterized by the pervasiveness of transnational linkages, spillovers, and contagions. States are essential partners in what have been called "global public policy networks" that seek to deal with modern, complex issues (Reinicke et al. 2001), such as climate change, migration, and management of the global commons such as oceans.

As participants in broader global regimes, states are sovereign, or putatively autonomous, but in practical terms they are often one participant among many in international systems of norms, monitoring, and participation in compliance, together with international and inter-governmental organizations, transnational NGOs, and civil society. The modern view of the state is one in which sovereignty is "shared" or embedded in an international global order, one explicitly oriented toward protection of its citizens from direct and indirect security threats, with responsibilities to protect human rights and obligations to create the conditions for development and prosperity.

As the 2005 UN High-level Panel on Threats, Challenges, and Change concluded:

> If there is to be a new security consensus, it must start with the understanding that the front-line actors in dealing with all the threats we face, new and old, continue to be individual sovereign States, whose role and responsibilities, and right to be respected, are fully recognized in the Charter of the United Nations. But in the twenty-first century, more than ever before, no State can stand wholly alone. Collective strategies, collective institutions and a sense of collective responsibility are indispensable.[11]

CHAPTER THREE

International Engagement for Statebuilding after Civil War

Because a poorly governed or captured state is a strong initial driver of fragility, recovery of state capacities through international assistance has emerged as a leitmotif of international responses. Why "statebuilding?" The term and practice of statebuilding emerged in the late 1990s and early 2000s in response to frustration with what were found to be myopic peacebuilding approaches to post-war environments of the early 1990s, which relied on rapid political transitions and quick elections as a way to restore governance functions in post-war countries ... allowing international peacekeeping forces to exit. The peacebuilding approaches in Cambodia, El Salvador, Mozambique, and Namibia drew on models of "democratization" combined with an "exit strategy" mentality to international intervention (Caplan 2012).

While the democratization-and-exit approach was initially successful in some cases (Namibia and Mozambique are often cited as important early successes), the approach ran aground with the recurrence of war in Angola in 1992 following a failed, rushed attempt at elections, and later – with tragedy – as the peace process in Rwanda in 1994 collapsed into a genocide that the UN failed to prevent and arrest. Similarly, what started as a one-year occupation of Bosnia in 1995 has turned into a now 15-year transitional administration as early attempts to stitch together an effective state foundered on lingering ethnic tensions and fears of conflict relapse. Scholars who studied these initial post-Cold War interventions to build peace after civil war decried the international approach of rapid elections and market-oriented economic reforms as ill-conceived, arguing instead for an "institutionalization before democratization," or statebuilding, alternative (Paris 2004: 189–207). The example of Timor-Leste, too, illustrates how the international community intervened to arrest conflict and state collapse following the referendum on independence from Indonesia in 1999, held elections, and then withdrew peacekeepers . . . only to re-deploy foreign troops after violence re-erupted in 2006. These initial failings of a simplistic "liberal peace" model to building peace after civil war are the origin of the contemporary focus on statebuilding today and inform how the statebuilding issue emerged on the international security and development agenda (Chesterman et al. 2004).

The focus on statebuilding also has its origin in the realization that restoration or creation of governance institutions and processes at the national, regional, and local level is an essential ingredient for consolidating the peace . . . "consolidation" is indeed the antonym to "fragility." Without security, there cannot be effective long-term development, yet without development and the mitigation of deeply entrenched poverty, security is unlikely to be forthcoming (Tschirgi et al. 2010). Neither security nor development can be advanced in the long term without an autonomous, authoritative, legitimate, and capable state. Thus, the statebuilding approach resides at the intersection between traditional security approaches, such as military intervention, stabilization, and security sector reform, and long-term development agendas, such as enabling macro-economic growth and providing essential public goods or services (such as clean water, health care, and education).

International responses to war and post-war contexts have evolved in parallel with the contexts and the requirements of peacemaking, peacebuilding, and long-term development of governance capacities. As above, one of the lessons learned from recent experience has been that the emphasis on "quick fixes," such as rapid implementation of peace agreement provisions and early elections, is fallacious. Liberal approaches to statebuilding – emphasizing democracy and participation, contestation in electoral processes, human rights, together with the state as the guarantor of private markets – have been deeply challenged in the scholarly and practitioner debates (Newman et al. 2009). In this view, characteristic of earlier responses was a hurried and sometimes misplaced focus on exit strategies. The concept of "exit strategies" – often tied to electoral events as the end of transitional processes – has since been rethought and is now more accurately described as the goal of "peace consolidation," with statebuilding increasingly seen as the linchpin priority in achieving long-lasting peace.[1]

Common to these earlier experiences of peacebuilding was the reliance on a linear formula or model for consolidating peace in post-war settings: a first phase, in which security restructuring occurs and in which external peacekeepers provide security as emergency relief is provided, disarmament occurs, and transitional governments are established and rule; a second phase of transition, in which elections occur, new constitutions are drafted and ratified, and the country is stabilized; and a third phase, in which a continued international presence assists in the amelioration of root causes of conflict through economic development and further democratization (Dobbins et al. 2005). These tasks are neatly outlined in the United States Department of State's "Essential Tasks Matrix," which features a list of short-, medium-, and long-term imperatives for post-war stabilization and reconstruction ranging from territorial security to community rebuilding.[2]

The best-laid plans, however, run aground in the messy realities of war-torn countries, as the US Army learned in Iraq and Afghanistan, where conventional measures for benchmarking progress in the restoration of state capacities – despite unprecedented investments of money and manpower – proved to provide misleading information.[3] At least one lesson learned is that external support for internal statebuilding is a complex, delicate, and uncertain endeavor, and that sometimes local actors can out-manipulate and indeed out-maneuver the internationals (Barnett and Zuercher 2009). And there are deep and inherent tensions in balancing the short-term needs of early recovery and of transitional peace-building with the longer-term goals of statebuilding, which need to be understood and acknowledged.[4] Consolidating peace is not simply a matter of rebuilding state capacity based on what was there before, or "recovery;" statebuilding is about transformation of both state and society. Moreover, aid statebuilding support does not lead, as Charles Call suggests, "directly and unproblematically" to peace, due to the strategic risks inherent in backing some social forces over others or in practical risks such as corruption (2008: 366).

Pathways from War to Peace

There is a yawning gap between the idealized notion of what a modern, twenty-first-century state should be and the realities of governments on the ground in war-torn countries. It is impossible to begin evaluating the statebuilding debates today without an appreciation for the path-dependent nature of various starting points or pathways to peace in the variety of contexts seen among the countries listed in tables 1.1 and 1.2; there is a fallacy in the scholarly literature and policy circles to make generalizations about post-war countries without consideration of the terms and conditions on which a war unfolds and how it ends. *How* a war ends is a critical point of departure in the debates on contemporary statebuilding.

For example, perhaps the most facilitative context for

statebuilding – in terms of authority, at least – is when there is a clear military victory, such as the definitive overthrow of the Qadhafi regime in 2011 by NATO-backed rebels, or the unilateral victory by the Ethiopian People's Revolutionary Democratic Front (EPRDF) over the Ethiopian state in 1991, or the success of the Rwanda Patriotic Front in taking power after the genocidal violence of 1994 (to name a few). With military victory, there are no messy compromises needed with the former regime, and the state can be remade to serve the statebuilding visions of the victorious elites . . . these regimes, from the outset, have greater degrees of autonomy and may be less prone to war recurrence (Toft 2010). However, while military victories may facilitate the consolidation of state power, often that power is abused and post-war governments can slip into authoritarianism (as in Ethiopia, or as is often alleged in Sri Lanka and Rwanda). Statebuilding in countries such as Sri Lanka, Uganda, and Rwanda, where war ended through a one-sided military victory, are quite different from those that ended in negotiated settlements and heavy-footprint peace-keeping deployments such as in Bosnia, Burundi, or Liberia. For example, Sabine Kurtenbach argues that, historically, states in Latin America were more effectively built after military victories than those that ended in negotiated settlements which tend to leave instability in their wake (Kurtenbach 2011).

Historically, we know that by far most civil wars do in fact end in victory of one side over the other.[5] Barbara Walter has similarly analyzed war termination through comprehensive analysis, and she reports that between 1940 and 1990, only 20 percent of civil wars ended in negotiations (Walter 1997). Contrary to these historical trends, however, of the major civil wars of the post-Cold War period, nearly half (47 percent according to Mack 2007) of those no longer active have ended in comprehensive peace agreements. Trends in patterns of war termination changed dramatically in the post-Cold War era and these trends pose new questions for thinking about statebuilding and the variety of starting points that are seen. In 1998, Wallensteen and Sollenberg reported that of the 108 conflicts since 1989, 75 had ended by 1998. "Of these," they write, "21 were ended by peace agreements, whereas 24 ended in victory for one of the sides and 30 had other outcomes (cease-fire agreements or activity below the level for inclusion). Many new peace agreements were signed in the middle and late parts of the period, particularly during 1995–96" (Wallensteen and Sollenberg 1998: 597).

In wars ended by peace agreement, such accords (or "pacts") typically reflect the dynamics of conflict in power structures and institutions such that it is difficult to move beyond the war-ending agreement to create a state that can transcend war-time enmities. This is the situation in Lebanon, where the 1989 Ta'if Agreement left intact the sectarian power-sharing formula of the state, and which many see as the basis for continued fragility in that country that has in turn inhibited development and the consolidation of peace through an authoritative, legitimate, and capable state.[6]

In other cases, efforts to achieve negotiated settlements are partial and leave "quasi-states" in an international legal limbo. The Oslo Agreement of 1993 in the Israeli–Palestinian conflict has set the stage for statebuilding in Palestine following the two-state solution for this protracted conflict, which has yielded some success in creating the edifice of what could be an independent Palestinian state.[7] However, the full enjoyment of recognition or sovereignty and full control of the Palestinian-governed territory of Gaza under the Hamas faction remains outside of the Palestinian Authority's control. Likewise, continued international disagreement on the status of Kosovo reveals the sometimes partial and indeterminate nature of authority in the post-war period; Kosovo has a state, but its recognition is limited and it does not yet enjoy full international backing for its status as an independent state.

This discussion suggests the need for a concise understanding and typology of starting points for statebuilding based on the path dependency of war-ending outcomes.[8] I suggest these five categories, which reflect starkly different starting points for thinking about statebuilding after contemporary civil wars.

- First, there is *statebuilding from scratch*. That is, the enterprise of creating a wholly new state in situations where state institutions and processes are in territories previously ruled by another state, such as in Kosovo or Timor-Leste.
- Second, there is statebuilding in *contexts of destroyed state capacity*, where the state was rendered fully disabled, but where there are antecedents to prior functionality (such as an extant legal code or some local structures) and in some instances continuity in key ministries or in sectors such as the police forces, as in Afghanistan, Democratic Republic of Congo, Haiti, Somalia, or Iraq.
- Third, there is statebuilding following war in which *the state was previously captured* by a party to the conflict in an essentially predatory or exclusive way, as in Central African Republic, Guatemala, Liberia, Libya, and Nepal.
- Fourth, there is statebuilding in *contexts where the state is shared*, but contested, in which continuing social differences or conflict limits state effectiveness and the government is constituted as a power-sharing system, as in Bosnia, Burundi, or Lebanon.
- Finally, there are *contexts of only partial state formation*, such as in Palestine or Kosovo, where the state continues to be limited by the absence of a comprehensive peace agreement and universal external recognition of the state.

The list is by no means exhaustive, nor are the examples given mutually exclusive. This typology, at best, suggests that the statebuilding concept itself is elastic and imprecise and that there are no simple "state in a box" solutions. For example, one can see statebuilding themes in the creation of sub-national units where peace settlements have yielded high degrees of autonomy for such units and the creation or restoration of regional government within a broader state is the goal, such as the Kurdistan Regional Government in Iraq or the provincial/decentralized government in Indonesia/Aceh that was the outcome of the conflict in that context. The important point is that before one begins a broader debate about the possibilities, and limits, of statebuilding in any given context, it is critical to begin with a clearer understanding of the points of post-war departure and the varieties of context to which the term relates.

Debating International Statebuilding: Shared Sovereignty?

Some skeptics of the international enterprise to use intervention and aid flows to rebuild the state after war have gone further to argue that no intervention may well be the best approach. Jeremy Weinstein has argued that what may be best for war-torn countries is "autonomous recovery" without outside help, and that the international community as a whole has often overstretched the assumption that intervention is mostly helpful (2005). Backing the scholarship that shows that military victories can lead to more durable peace, and referencing the scholarship on endogenous statebuilding in Europe, the implication is that sometimes it is best to back a winner strongly committed to statebuilding rather than pursuing inclusive peace agreements through "peacemaking." Citing cases like Uganda, Eritrea, and the autonomous (but unrecognized) province of Somaliland, Weinstein argues that sometimes little or no intervention yields more satisfactory results than does the "aided" statebuilding approach.

Despite this argument, intervention in civil war and post-civil war settings occurs anyway, in part because of the spillover effects of civil war for international society (outlined in chapter 1). For this reason, we can explain the in-between space of international intervention and local ownership as one of "shared" sovereignty between international actors and local elites (Krasner 2004); international intervention, be it military or through development aid, restricts domestic state autonomy. This is true most poignantly in cases where sovereignty is held solely by the United Nations in transitional administrations (in which the UN assumes temporary or transitional authority over a territory), as in Bosnia, Eastern Slavonia, Kosovo, or East Timor (in its transition to Timor-Leste). Statebuilding outcomes under transitional administrations have been disappointing; they seem subject to crisis and reversal (Caplan 2005; Chesterman 2004). Today, it is recognized that statebuilding is still – as historically – an essentially internally driven process, and that the most appropriate role for outsiders is to facilitate and support capacity through military intervention such as peacekeeping, UN "political missions" as in Iraq, Afghanistan, or Nepal, and through post-war aid flows.[9]

Indeed, the issues of statebuilding in fragile states is at the top of the development community's agenda precisely because of the enormous amounts of aid targeted to the fragile states, which receive more than 50 percent of the world's total overseas development assistance of the OECD countries. Most of the money is spent, precariously, in the top six aid recipient states, which also happen to be those that are highly fragile: Afghanistan, Ethiopia, Iraq, West Bank and Gaza, Sudan, Uganda, and the DRC (in order of total aid, 2008). The OECD-DAC reports that:

> In 2009, official development assistance to fragile states increased in real terms by USD 3.8 billion (+ 11%) to USD 40.5 billion. This represents a third of all aid flows to develop-

ing countries in this same year and accounts for 36% of the total increase in ODA between 2008 and 2009. However, 51% of aid is benefiting just 6 of the 41 countries in 2009, while 15 fragile states witnessed absolute declines between 2008 and 2009. A similar trend can be seen among bilateral donors beyond the DAC, where a reported USD 1.1 billion in aid – 20% of the total – went to fragile states in 2009, but where 60% went to just three fragile states (OECD-DAC 2010b: 2).

There are several serious criticisms about the ability of the international community to employ aid – money and technical help – to advance what are essentially internal political processes of consolidation of authority and the building of state capacity. One concern is that outsiders often lack a common strategy and seem unable to coordinate in such a way as to create the right incentives for local protagonists to build capable institutions. Second, resources – specialists, infrastructure needs, and capital – are often insufficient, or, conversely, overwhelming of the context and thus create aid dependencies. Third, there are those that suggest aid flows create incentives for local leaders and bureaucrats of states to be more loyal to the donors than to their own people. Even more nefarious, some – such as David Chandler in his analysis of the statebuilding approach applied to post-war Bosnia – see international statebuilding as ultimately injurious and neglectful of local desires and realities (Chandler 2006).

Dilemmas in Policy and Practice

Various scholarly projects have tended to confirm that international intervention to build states internally is fraught with inherent dilemmas of approach and action, rendering sequential or roadmap approaches to statebuilding limited at best. Paris and Sisk (2009), drawing on the findings of a research team that investigated military intervention, aid, and democratization, among other topics, found five principal types of dilemmas that confront international actors seeking to build states in post-war contexts.

- First, *temporal dilemmas* occur in which short-term requirements for stability and peace may work against longer-term requirements for the underlying social, political, and economic transformations required to prevent future violence and to foster socio-economic development.
- Second, *dilemmas of authority* arise in which the international community may need to exercise a muscular security presence to ensure stability and peace; however, this serves to dis-empower local actors and create problems of neo-imperial overstretch, or, concomitantly, dependency on a continued international presence.
- Third, *dilemmas of participation* emerge when the international community engages primarily with elites (for example, in peacemaking negotiations); however, over time there must be popular involvement in reconstituting the polity if it is to be durable and legitimate.
- Fourth, *values-based dilemmas* arise when the international community, following its norms of participation and inclusion, pursue processes of liberalization (for example, the advancement of gender equality) that collide with local values and informal authority structures.
- And, finally, *systemic dilemmas appear* when there is a clash of interests and preferences between actors at the international level and those at the local level (Paris and Sisk 2009: 1–21).

Reflective of these dilemmas, scholars and practitioners have begun to recognize that there are real risks and potential for doing harm in supporting statebuilding, and debates swirl about how to best structure, sequence, coordinate, and prioritize international responses (OECD-DAC 2010a). Contemporary debates consider the efficacy and utility of the sequential and liberal peacebuilding approach as seen from international organizations – especially the UN – and especially over the extent to which the international community should strive to create a state that features "good enough" governance, "good" governance, or democracy as the ultimate goal of international engagement (see chapter 7). Much depends not only on what is desirable, but also what is feasible.

In rethinking approaches to external aid for statebuilding, the international community has grappled with a better understanding of how to effectively balance support for early recovery and initial restoration of government functions and the long-term needs for internal capacity and the gradual expansion of participation and inclusion. Benchmarks of progress include improved performance in the delivery of security and rule of law, transparent and accountable political governance, efficient public finance, and wider economic recovery.[10]

Success in these areas directly affects the capacity of the state to reinstate authority and enjoy domestic legitimacy. Progress on statebuilding does seem to require some basic political settlement to be successful: an agreed rules of the game for contention and bargaining among elites.[11] Yet with the persistence of war economy patterns, in which individuals focus on livelihoods and shadow economic structures control critical markets, violence and conflict can become incentivized. State actors may well benefit more from a lack of state capacity than from extending authority over these informal institutions that regulate war economies. Case-study analysis from Senegal (Casamance), Sierra Leone, and Eastern DRC shows how local-level incentives have created the patterns of persistent war economies and the systematic evasion of state authority as a core survival strategy for governing elites.[12] This concern has led donors to focus on tools such as "power analysis" that investigates the interactions of power between formal actors in the state and informal institutions and agents; particularly, such approaches look for structures and power relations in society that inhibit poverty reduction, fuel broader social frustration, and feed conflict dynamics, particularly in highly personalistic or "neo-patrimonial" regimes (Cammack 2007).

Similar in intent are "political economy" analysis methods that seek to discern the economic incentives of local protagonists, including at various levels of the state, and the ways in which incentive systems of economic accumulation affect the capacity of the state to have the will to govern effectively.[13] This perspective emphasizes the multiplicity of informal economic institutions that exist in fragile-state environments, how coalitions among ruling political elites are unstable, and how rent-seeking and patronage politics feeds into a weak-state syndrome. Understanding the basis of interactions and incentives of governing elites in turn should be the starting point for informing how donors can more effectively program aid to avoid such harmful practices as backing an illegitimate or at best partially legitimate state in ways that undermine the pursuit of long-term peace, and that they identify those agents and structures in society that can be contribute to positive change.[14]

Conclusion

Meaningful progress in restoring or recreating states in post-war countries is frequently bedeviled by liberal "orthodoxies" transplanted from consolidated, democratic countries. Challenges experienced in assistance based on a transplantation of Western models to post-war contexts include poor progress on reducing insecurities or promoting development, unintended outcomes, operational difficulties, lack of policy guidance and inapplicable tools to address contemporary dilemmas, and competing priorities in support of developing state capacities (OECD-DAC 2008).

External support for internal statebuilding is a highly political process, and recreating states is more than technical assistance to government institutions; statebuilding is a function of state–society relations. In its best form, statebuilding is an essentially domestic process driven by state–society relations that seeks to strengthen, build, or rebuild authority, capacity, and legitimacy of the state institutions in order to create the conditions necessary for institutions of security, and stable, transparent rules of the game to facilitate development.

Putting together an analysis of the nature and drivers of fragility and the concomitant approaches and tasks of post-war security and development suggests the need for an integrated organizing framework within which to think about the nature and scope of statebuilding tasks in post-war environments in a holistic way. Figure 3.1 provides such an organizing framework, drawing on both the conceptual orientation presented here and some of the more practice-oriented themes in the chapters that follow. This figure provides something of a roadmap to how the conceptual frameworks presented in this and the previous chapter relate to the more pragmatic and applied concerns of the chapters that follow.

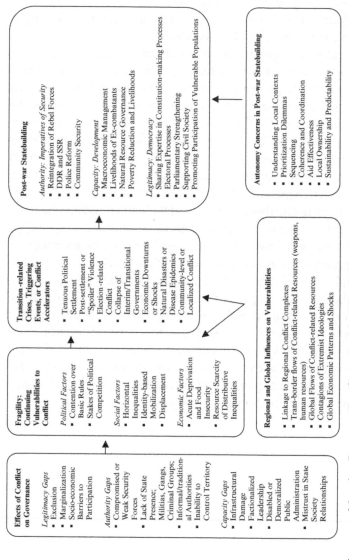

Effects of Conflict on Governance

Legitimacy Gaps
- Exclusion
- Marginalization
- Socio-economic Barriers to Participation

Authority Gaps
- Compromised or Weak Security Forces
- Lack of State Presence; Militias, Gangs, Criminal Groups; Informal/traditional Authorities
- Inability to Control Territory

Capacity Gaps
- Infrastructural Damage
- Factionalized Leadership
- Disabled or Demoralized Public Administration
- Mistrust in State Society Relationships

Fragility: Continuing Vulnerabilities to Conflict

Political Factors
- Contention over Basic Rules
- Stakes of Political Competition

Social Factors
- Horizontal Inequalities
- Identity-based Mobilization
- Displacement

Economic Factors
- Acute Deprivation and Food Insecurity
- Resource Scarcity of Distributive Inequalities

Regional and Global Influences on Vulnerabilities
- Linkage to Regional Conflict Complexes
- Trans-border flows of Conflict-related Resources (weapons, human resources)
- Global Flows of Conflict-related Resources
- Contagions of Extremist Ideologies
- Global Economic Patterns and Shocks

Transition-related Crises, Triggering Events, or Conflict Accelerators
- Tenuous Political Settlement
- Post-settlement or "Spoiler" Violence
- Election-related Conflict
- Collapse of Interim/Transitional Governments
- Economic Downturns or Shocks
- Natural Disasters or Disease Epidemics
- Community-level or Localized Conflict

Post-war Statebuilding

Authority: Imperatives of Security
- Reintegration of Rebel Forces
- DDR and SSR
- Police Reform
- Community Security

Capacity: Development
- Macroeconomic Management
- Livelihoods of Ex-combatants
- Natural Resource Governance
- Poverty Reduction and Livelihoods

Legitimacy: Democracy
- Sharing Expertise in Constitution-making Processes
- Electoral Processes
- Parliamentary Strengthening
- Supporting Civil Society
- Promoting Participation of Vulnerable Populations

Autonomy Concerns in Post-war Statebuilding
- Understanding Local Contexts
- Prioritization Dilemmas
- Sequencing
- Coherence and Coordination
- Aid Effectiveness
- Local Ownership
- Sustainability and Predictability

Figure 3.1: Mapping Post-war Fragility to Statebuilding Objectives

CHAPTER FOUR

Authority: Imperatives of Security

Insecurity is at the heart of fragility, and restoring security or securing it may be the most difficult part of the statebuilding puzzle. There are both intrinsic and instrumental reasons to focus on security as a first priority. Intrinsically, to advance security is to save lives from violent conflict and its effects, and to prevent the emergence of a predatory state which itself threatens the security of its citizens. Instrumentally, security is a prerequisite for development and to give opportunity for societies to resolve conflicts through non-violent processes such as constitution-making processes and elections. Security today is seen as a comprehensive problem in terms of the scope of the issues, from the transition from external security by peacekeepers or occupiers to local forces, disarmament, demobilization, and reintegration of rebel factions and government soldiers, security sector reform (SSR) of national military doctrines, removing landmines, reform and professionalization of armies and police forces, anti-terrorism, and through a community-level and indeed urban-level approach (especially in countries with large mega-cities experiencing high levels of political or criminal violence, such as Lagos in Nigeria or Guatemala City in Guatemala).[1]

The challenges to reconstituting security in the wake of violent conflict are myriad. Countries emerging from conflict often feature a bloated military – a product of war-time mobilization – and often expansion of the army if rebel forces are to be integrated into the ranks when required under peace agreements. The difficulties of integration of combatants who had previously fought as enemies cannot be overstated, and the challenges of security sector reform are both deep and broad. Strengthening the security sector must also be accompanied by the strengthening of institutions of accountability, meaning the loyalty and deference of military elites to civilian authorities, and the accountability of civilian authority to institutions of the rule of law. To achieve accountability, the process of security transformation involves not only the reform of armed forces, but overhauling an entire infrastructure of the justice system, such as courts, prisons, and practical aspects like promulgation of new firearms laws (Brozka 2006).

Ultimately, the aims of security sector reform are political: to transform erstwhile rebels into political actors and broaden the basis of the social contract with the state of long-disaffected communities. For this reason, security must be seen in terms of both the political elements of insurgent reintegration and broader social consensus on the legitimacy of the state, and it must navigate the intensely political issues such as the disarmament, demobilization, and reintegration (DDR) of former rebel forces. Security is contingent on the commitment of the protagonists in conflict; the UN Capstone Doctrine on peacekeeping – often deployed to substitute for failed-state capacity – reflects the realization that progress in security allowing for international exit and restoration of local autonomy is contingent on essentially political conditions:

> A traditional United Nations peacekeeping operation can be said to have successfully completed its mandate once the states concerned have arrived at a mutually agreed settlement to their conflict. Since they have little direct involvement in diplomatic efforts to resolve the conflict, some traditional peacekeeping operations are deployed for decades, due to the absence of a lasting political settlement between the parties.[2]

Here we evaluate the emerging lessons learned from international efforts to restore the state's authority through a more comprehensive look at the reform of security institutions and local structures for preventing conflicts from escalating into violence, and at crisis management and dispute resolution at the local level. The security agenda in today's fragile states is also about limiting and abating political violence, curbing local and transnational crime syndicates, and preventing violence against women, girls, and other especially vulnerable populations (such as international migrants). Indeed, much of contemporary thinking on peace consolidation focuses on the extent to which security sector reform has progressed and the vulnerability of society to new violence has diminished.

When States Fail: Imperatives of International Intervention

Barbara Walter (1997) has insightfully shown that providing security in the wake of war is best done when outsiders can deploy forces as a way of providing credible commitment to wary protagonists who at war's end fear that peace will be but a pause in conflict. The notion of "credible commitment" applies especially to those cases of negotiated settlements, where the fears of parties defecting from peace deals and returning to the battlefield seem most acute. Similarly, Virginia Page Fortna has shown that peacekeeping works: countries are less likely to slip into recurrent conflict if there has been a UN peace operation deployed (2004b), findings that reaffirm earlier research by Doyle and Sambanis (2000) The deployment of robust or strong international peacekeeping operations to facilitate transitions from war to peace has been seen as a viable and indeed cost-effective way for the international community to help create conditions of stability on the ground and begin the process of reforming security sector institutions and de-militarizing societies through police reform (United Nations Department of Peacekeeping Operations 2009).

However, it is important to emphasize that the achievement of a reformed security sector in governance is very much a function of the extent to which the new regime is broadly perceived as legitimate. Security is not just the provision of national, group-based, or personal security by force in new state; it is also the political legitimacy of the government that in turn generates trust from society. Security, in sum, is to some extent a function of the depth and durability of the political settlement, that is the extent to which there is consensus among elites over a particular formula concerning the legitimacy of the state (such as a war-terminating peace agreement) (Whaites 2008). Post-war statebuilding requires the demilitarization of politics, in which parties agree to forego the battlefield for the administrative authority of a state that is held accountable, regulated by the rule of law, and in which military and police functions are distinct from internal political interests (Giddens 1987; Lyons 2005).

In the early phases of international intervention, the focus turns to "stabilization." A prior question in intervention to achieve international security is the mandate and size of international deployments. Some argue in favor of a heavy footprint – extensive international deployments that no local protagonist could reasonably challenge, drawing on the doctrine of "overwhelming forces." However, a heavy footprint can engender local hostility, particularly when international forces unintentionally target civilians, or when outside forces misbehave and unruly foreign troops engage in criminal activity or sexual violence. Over time, no country's population wants to be ruled by foreigners – even ostensibly neutral UN peacekeepers – and thus international intervention tends to experience an obsolescing bargain, where the initial welcome of outsiders in bringing the peace wanes over time (Edelstein 2009).

A heavy footprint by international forces is more likely in the most devastated societies – where international forces substitute for the presence of local security capacities – versus a light footprint as a way of engendering more local ownership. There are also questions of sequencing of approaches, such as the early deployment of an international coalition of the willing and the hand-off to the United Nations in Haiti. The timeframe needed for reform and transformation of the security sector often exceeds what is practically or politically feasible in terms of deployment of international peace operations.

The resurgence of the Taliban in Afghanistan in the late 2000s, for example, continues to pose a rival source of authority and extraction in the country in competition with the fledgling, internationally backed regime of Afghanistan President Hamid Karzai, brought to power after post-9/11 military intervention in 2001. While these examples underscore the threat to security for incipient statebuilding enterprises, they are not typical of countries that are emerging from war through negotiated peace agreements. In this case, security sector reform guided by outsiders is about strengthening the state against potential challengers, and insulating the state's capacity to coerce from capture by one or more of the parties.

Barnett Rubin argues that when the state is weak or contested, preventing the relapse into war requires that international intervening forces have legitimacy, can bring economic returns, and can provide capital for financing security sector reform; he argues that negotiating the security transition is in fact more important than negotiating the political transition (Rubin 2008: 44). He argues that in Afghanistan "despite frequently agreeing to succumb to civilian political authorities, armed factions (including government and armed forces) often fortify parallel or existing command or authority structures to weaken the actual power of nominal civilian control" (2008: 38).

A key question is therefore whether and to what extent the government itself has legitimacy and has the capacity to actually prevail over armed non-state forces. In some cases, co-opted elites retain their capacity for coercion outside the state while pledging to disarm. For example, in Lebanon, UN Security Council Resolution 1559 calls for the disarmament of non-state actors such as Hezbollah. In Nepal, the process has involved integration of former Maoist guerillas into a new, reformed Nepalese national army, whereas in Colombia the process has been one of dismantling paramilitary organizations. Yet in the Nepal case, despite the completion of reintegration, the consolidation of peace remains incomplete until a new constitution is finalized.

When the state is weak or contested, and the chance for renewed return to war is evident, there is indeed a strong argument in favor of an overwhelming forces approach. Heavy-footprint deployments such as IFOR/SFOR/EUFOR in Bosnia as a coalition force – or more recently in Liberia with the deployment of UN peacekeepers through the United Nations Mission in Libera (UNMIL) – have seen success in preventing what may well have been recurrences of conflict. The heavy-footprint approach has at least kept the peace, even if it has at times frustrated local ownership. In Bosnia, there have been no fatalities among NATO peacekeeping troops from hostilities, and although the country is not integrated or consolidated as a state, there has been no repeat of the deep violence that gripped the country in the civil war of 1992–95. Likewise, in Liberia, UNMIL has been credited with keeping the peace – and helping stabilize the region – in the war-torn country through two electoral processes, while at the same time serving as the principal coordinator of the training up of a new Liberian army and, in this context most importantly, a new police force.

Heavy-footprint missions are not just a function of their size, but also of the legitimacy and rules of engagement that are found in the mandates of the United Nations Security Council under Chapter VII of the Charter. Legitimacy for the imposition of security comes from outside, primarily from the Security Council. Yet ultimately, as the UN peacekeeping Capstone Doctrine realistically notes, their success depends on those very local actors to accept the intervention as neutral and credible and to achieve their own political settlement. The advantages of UN peacekeeping in creating initial conditions of security – in substituting for the state's capacity, essentially – are significant. In addition to the provision of credible commitment to peace agreements, UN forces are generally more broadly legitimate externally and internally; when backed by strong international power, they may also have the longer-term staying power needed to create stability in the most difficult environments.

The cases of Afghanistan, Bosnia, Haiti, and Timor-Leste all illustrate in their own way the need for a long-term presence of external forces to provide for security moving along a heavy to light spectrum. Long-term commitments like these and in cases like Liberia, however, may be an exception in the sense that most peacekeeping missions today are inadequately funded and staffed, there is a shortage of truly capable, trained, professional peacekeepers, and there remains strong pressures (sometimes from host governments, as in the DRC) for early withdrawal of UN peacekeepers. Peacekeeping is in a rolling crisis, where the demands tend to exceed the supply of troops, and partnerships among organizations still prove inadequate in matching global "demand" for peacekeeping with the deployment of sufficiently robust missions (such as the NATO–African Union partnership to aid the deployment of UN troops in Darfur, or UNAMID) (International Peace Institute 2009; Geneva Center for Security Policy 2010).

Moreover, the mandates for peacekeeping have grown, to include early efforts to engage in statebuilding. The deployment of multidimensional peace operations in the 1990s (with roles to organize elections, observe and advance human rights, and restore the basic functions of governance) has grown ever wider. Security Council mandates for missions have grown from an initial minimal approach of providing security for humanitarian relief – an approach which was seen as being at the heart of the failure of the UN Protection Force in Bosnia during the war (UNPROFOR) – to today's more robust mandates that allow both defensive force by peacekeepers (in defense of themselves) and offensive force to take on spoilers or recalcitrant parties (in defense of the mandate). In the Democratic Republic of Congo, for example, the UN mission (MONUSCO) has engaged in offensive military action in the eastern regions in pursuit of rebel forces who have challenged the peace and who have engaged in gross violations of human rights such as the mass rape of women and the kidnapping of child soldiers. Overall, Chapter VII mandates from the Security Council for peacekeeping now include both the authorization for offensive military action (so-called "robust" peacekeeping) and mandate that external forces help protect civilians from atrocities. This mandate has proven especially difficult to achieve in many of the UN operations in Africa, for example, given the depth of state fragility in many of these contexts such as in DRC or South Sudan, where threats to civilian populations come from rebel forces and state-allied militaries and militias alike.[3]

It is for these reasons that peacekeeping doctrine has evolved away from a primarily military mission to one in which the civilian components – designed especially toward statebuilding objectives – have become central. Peacekeeping cannot be successful without a political vision which includes advancing a political settlement on which the state is based and which sets the stage for the state's eventual ability to provide for its own security and the security of its citizens. This broadening of the peacekeeping mission has put the emphasis on two core aspects related to statebuilding. The first is the need to engage early with an international policing presence which can provide essential monitoring and training for a reconstructed police and internal security force that is able to secure the country's borders to provide for regional stabilization. Complementary to, or in some cases in the absence of, a military force, deploying armed but not militarily capable police may be worse than doing nothing at all; comparative experience shows that monitors and police units are especially vulnerable members of peace operations when the combatants are much more heavily armed.[4]

Deployment of formed international police units has also been the basis for international engagement in Nepal, where due to local ownership constraints (Nepali nationalism) and regional sensitivities (particularly the views of India), the United Nations Mission in Nepal (UNMIN) was a primarily political mission but did include formed United Nations civilian police units. This "light footprint" approach has been praised by some who see it as a model alternative to the heavy intervention that portends more risks for international engagement (Suhrke 2011). Detractors argue that political and light-footprint approaches are often insufficient in providing credible commitment, may pose risks when internationals lack the ability to protect themselves, and they cannot possibly address the demands of immediate verification of containment and demobilization of forces (which has been an issue in Nepal).

Unarmed or lightly armed observers may make a difference if there is sufficient internal monitoring capability by domestic capacities (e.g., civil society groups) and a group of military and police officers willing and able to quickly form the basis of a neutral, committed, uncorrupted internal security and policing force. Famously, the all-female battalion of Indian military police in Liberia has been seen as a model of how sympathetic outsiders can constructively contribute to security; the UNMIL female UN police have been praised, especially, for being able to work with women who have suffered from conflict or who continue to face personal insecurities in the post-war period, as Liberia continues to see relatively high levels of gender-based violence.[5]

What is clear is that peacekeeping today needs to be augmented by early attention to the statebuilding perspective. It is in the early stages of military intervention when short-term considerations such as "winning hearts and minds" of the locals through quick impact projects are delivered by internationals. This approach, together with those such as provincial reconstruction teams (where the military begins to do development work; see chapter 5, p. 109), may have the effect of undermining the credibility of the state as a service provider and failing to create sufficient local ownership of the reconstruction process. As well, there have been continuing tensions between robust peacekeeping efforts and the countervailing principle of neutrality in the provision of humanitarian relief. As a result, tensions between peacekeepers conducting peace enforcement missions and neutral humanitarian service providers have been seen in a number of settings, such as the DRC, where the values of saving lives and robust intervention by peacekeepers to expand state authority seem to collide.

Ultimately, the success of international missions is contingent on the extent to which security can provide space for the working of a transitional or interim government, which can organize a process of statebuilding based on negotiation over constitutional reform, early recovery of the economy and the restoration of livelihoods, and negotiating the exit of international forces.

Disarmament, Demobilization, and Reintegration

The disarmament, demobilization, and reintegration (DDR) of combatants are typical provisions in peace accords that foresee the reconstruction and transformation of security forces after war. Disarmament refers to the collection (and, usually, destruction) of war-time weapons, demobilization is about the cantonment and discharge of fighters, and reintegration is related to either their incorporation into restructured national police and armed forces or their discharge and return to society.[6] Typically, in peace agreements rebel forces agree to forgo waging the conflict through the gun for the non-violent contention of politics through their transformation into political parties, such that the origins of DDR terms and conditions are found in prior processes of negotiating peace agreements.

Thus, the opportunities for DDR in pursuit of peace are pivotal (Spear 2006). In cases where security sector reform (SSR) and DDR are part and parcel of a comprehensive peace agreement, programming in DDR is more explicit; in those instances where political integration is not a directly stated national goal (as in the case of military victories or regime change, as in the example of Iraq below), then DDR processes must take into account implicitly the political dimensions of reintegration. DDR processes, often combined with the reintegration of national military forces or the creation of new ones – to include armed forces as well as the police – can enable ex-combatants from (irregular) armed groups to make the critical shift from participation by the gun to participation through political parties, local associations, regional and local political institutions, and in issue-specific forums of policy making and implementation.

DDR is invariably highly political, and there is direct relationship between the success of the DDR process and the recovery of authority by the state in the political settlement (Ball and Van de Goor 2006). Indeed, Peter Swarbrick has argued in his study of DDR (and myriad related programs) in the DRC that the single most important factor for success in DDR is the concomitant political process; he writes that "The prime determinant of those conditions is usually the political situation, which, especially in the kinds of highly fluid and dynamic peacekeeping operations that have become the norm, is usually shifting very rapidly" (2006: 28). In sum, DDR is part of the overarching political strategy to induce armed actors to exchange violence for dialogue and accommodation through power sharing and electoral participation, and to re-establish the authority of a legitimate state to exercise accountably a monopoly in the use of violence; as such, it is inextricably linked with SSR (McFate 2010). In some cases, such as Afghanistan, the DRC, or Iraq, international interveners attempt to carry out DDR processes even when the fighting is still ongoing.

Today, the challenge of reintegration of ex-combatants is seen across a variety of conflict contexts, from historical early successes such the transformation of RENAMO (Mozambique National Resistance Organization) rebels into a political party in 1993 to the more contemporary challenges of integrating the FNL (Front for National Liberation) into the complex power-sharing and statebuilding processes in modern-day Burundi (Lemarchand 2006). If the transition from war to peace is about expanding the political space to include formerly armed and organized opposition, the political aspects of DDR are essential preconditions to progress. DDR is an essential step in the "de-militarization" of politics in post-war countries, and it is often critical that such processes unfold before other elements of transitions, particularly elections (Lyons 2005). Much has been learned about the technical aspects of DDR, including the issues of identification of combatants, addressing their economic and psychological needs, and providing for their return to civil life and reintegration into society. Indeed, the UN is now in its fourth generation of guidelines on the conduct of DDR programs, known as the Integrated Disarmament, Demobilization and Reintegration Standards (IDDRS) that outline guidance to practitioners and which highlight the complexity and sensitivities of the process.[7]

Disarmament of rebel fighters can either be through consensus, or DDR programs can be coercive: much depends on the process of war termination (see chapter 3). In cases of peace agreements, such as in Nepal in 2006, DDR takes place as part of a broader process of negotiating a political transition toward reform of the state and democratization, and as in many other instances the DDR process is also closely linked to SSR. In cases of military victory, DDR is often compulsory and carried out by the victors or by intervening international forces, with a stronger emphasis on lustration (vetting of those who committed war-time atrocities) and the complete disbandment of the rebel force.

A recurrent issue in disarmament is the question of verification of arms collection and compliance with peace agreements. In Northern Ireland, following the 1998 Belfast Agreement, a special independent international verification commission was created to ensure that Irish Republican Army stockpiles were put beyond use (called "decommissioning" in this context) and, eventually, destroyed.[8] The Northern Ireland case, however, is contrasted with those contexts such as Afghanistan or Somalia where the entire society is awash with weapons and it is quite difficult to distinguish between tools of war and guns for "traditional" uses, such as hunting (Small Arms Survey 2003: 288). In many cases, owning a weapon has become a survival tool, and this reality frustrates the goals of disarmament in highly insecure societies.

Demobilization involves the disbanding of military and paramilitary units (including rebels and, for example in the case of the Colombia, government-aligned vigilante groups). Such processes, which have been carried out in dozens of post-war countries since the 1990s, often involve the collection or cantonment of cadres, and programs through which they are prepared through vocational and educational programs to re-enter society. In many cases, where there are large numbers of child soldiers or female ex-combatants, demobilization programs have involved special efforts to address the particular needs of these populations. In Nepal, for example, nearly 20,000 former Maoist fighters were cantoned (brought together in camps), and in addition to former fighters those in cantonment camps include a high number of children born to fighters during the conflict, and more than 7,000 female ex-combatants. Thus, DDR goes well beyond a military enterprise and often involves attention to the social, psychological, and educational needs of "associated groups" such as ex-combatants' wives and children.

The transformation of armed groups is particularly fraught with dilemmas and challenges: scholarly research shows that often groups will only disarm and demobilize after a political process has progressed (for example, an election or recognition of independence). Comparative research findings suggest that DDR should come before the finalization of "final status" issues in peace negotiations (Höglund 2008). Their own security is paramount; without a sense of security in the post-war phase, fighters are often unwilling to risk disarmament and a return to an uncertain civilian life (Berdal and Ucko 2009). In complex and uncertain post-war processes, ex-combatant political motives, status, and role in politics is critical: commanders and other opposition elites must be assured of continuity in their position in a post-war government, mid-level commanders and senior non-commissioned personnel must see a future that does not compromise their core security or survival, and younger recruits must understand the overall political rationale for demobilization and the need for national unity, reconciliation, and peaceful politics (Muggah 2009). This has been a critical issue in the sometimes fraught DDR process in Liberia, in which the UN Mission in Liberia disarmed and demobilized more than 100,000 ex-combatants, including some 11,000 child soldiers (Jennings 2008). Many ex-combatants in Liberia have emerged as severely disaffected and frustrated, harboring deep grievances about the lack of compensation and opportunity for them in the post-war period.

The Liberia example raises a range of other concerns about reintegration: Will erstwhile cadres of soldiers re-form local political wings that, in the absence of economic opportunity, reconnect as criminal enterprises with political aims? This concern has been especially rife in those post-war countries where the lines between criminal and political violence have become deeply blurred in the post-war period, such as Côte d'Ivoire, Guatemala, Timor-Leste, and Burundi. DDR and small-arms control programs are often unable to effectively contend with post-war criminal and quasi-political violence (OECD-DAC 2009). This problem has been especially acute in the West Africa region, where transitional criminal gangs and cartels have infiltrated post-war countries characterized by weak governance to establish transit routes for drug smuggling into Western Europe, and in Kenya in the wake of the 2008–09 election-related violence.[9]

Reintegration often involves a dual transformation at the organizational (rebel-to-political party) and individual, ex-combatant levels (Söderberg Kovacs 2008). Organizational transformation involves the role of the DDR process for ex-combatants in terms of the motivation, capacity, and practice of political participation by ex-combatants from (irregular) armed groups to exercise rights and duties like any other citizen (Porto et al. 2007). The other aspect of the transformation is equally important: ex-combatants' roles change to become agents that act more as individuals within political parties than part of a top-down, hierarchical structure of military authority implying taking orders from rebel commanders. These dual transformations encompass much of the key issues that arise in the political implications of DDR programs. Leontine Specker argues that:

> Reintegration depends largely on two factors. First is the trust of ex-combatants in the (political) process. DDR cannot develop the political process, it needs to follow it. Second, the presence of economic alternatives is critical. DDR is fundamentally political in character and should be seen as part of a broader integrated approach to reconstruction processes, including security, governance, political and developmental aspects, requiring integrated context analyses and subsequent comprehensive strategy development (2008: 1).

While no context is the same, DDR processes offer both political risks and opportunities (Özerdem 2009). The risks are two-fold. First, the need for DDR is driven at the highest strategic level by the overall "recurrence" of conflict. The state-building imperative is often seen in the risk of aggrieved or mobilized ex-combatants abandoning the promise implicit in escaping conflict through an uncertain political transition and instead opting for a return to the more relative certainty of living by the gun. In Afghanistan, for example, NATO launched in 2003 the "New Beginnings" program designed to disarm and demobilize the Afghan Military Forces and to create the new Afghan National Army; the program, run by

UNDP, saw some 63,380 fighters demobilized, of which some 7,500 were child soldiers, and nearly 50,000 weapons were collected.[10]

The close and complex linkages between justice and peace-building inform the challenges of balancing transitional justice and political participation of ex-combatants in post-war countries. Often, a key to sustaining peace is ending impunity and ensuring accountability for war crimes and crimes against humanity (Goldstone 2004). This imperative is balanced against the need for reconciliation and for active participation in post-war politics, often for leaders of either armed forces or armed groups who have directly or indirectly committed crimes. For example, in Liberia, in the post-war legislature are erstwhile leaders such as Prince Johnson who openly attest to killing of political opponents in earlier periods. The primary linkage between DDR and transitional justice is that reintegration can contribute to the stability necessary to address human rights and rule of law, while addressing the need for truth, justice, and reparations can increase the legitimacy of reintegration programs that attempt to reintegrate ex-combatants into conflict-affected communities.

How transitional justice mechanisms can be success-fully integrated into DDR programs must be more explicitly addressed from the earliest planning stages.[11] For example, prosecutions may assist reintegration efforts by holding per-petrators of serious violations of human rights accountable under international law and, thereby, facilitate trust between ex-combatants and other citizens. Community and indi-vidual security may be adversely affected if perpetrators are reintegrated without sufficient investment in community security. Truth commissions may help reintegration efforts by promoting dialogue and reconciliation between ex-com-batants and victims. Reparations may promote reintegration efforts by demonstrating that aid is distributed in a balanced fashion to ex-combatants as well as to conflict-affected populations.

Security Sector Reform

At the top of the agenda in contexts of international statebuilding is the need to reform the security sector in the wake of conflict; often, the agreements on the nature of security sector reform or transformation are reached upstream in peace negotiations, as protagonists at peace talks typically have security at the top of their agendas as well. For example, in Burundi, power sharing in the military (at a ratio of 40 percent Tutsi, 60 percent Hutu) was a bargain that reflected the need to integrate the forces of the formerly Tutsi-dominated government with the mostly Hutu rebels.[12] The Burundi example is engaging as well because the combined force of integrated combatants was much larger that what a country the size of Burundi needs in terms of a standing army. Yet wholesale demobilization would be compromising of the peace given the concern that former ex-combatants would likely re-organize along ethnic lines: security sector reform, if done wrongly, would sow the seeds of a new insurgency.

Security reform in post-war countries is multi-layered and multi-faceted; moreover, historical contingencies often determine the structure of the security forces (for example, the relationship between the army, intelligence, internal security forces, and police). For example, in Sierra Leone, following the end of a more than decade-long civil war from 1991 to 2002, more than 50,000 fighters were demobilized from the rebel Revolutionary United Front (RUF), which had been accused of grave atrocities during the conflict. As Horn et al. (2006) have observed in their research on the Sierra Leone case, SSR is closely associated with two other areas central to the inherent difficulties of restoring authority in post-war statebuilding:

processes of transitional justice, and the creation of broader oversight and regulatory mechanisms to ensure that security forces are accountable and serve and have loyalty to the state, and not just serve the ruling regime. They report that the security sector reform process in Sierra Leone – involving both the restructuring and retraining of the police and the armed forces – was led by the United Kingdom and carried out under the auspices of the Commonwealth. Overall, the intensive four-year program was remarkably successful. They report that:

> The political, financial, logistical and security support provided by the UK government was, when supplemented by the limited resources of the Sierra Leone government, critical in securing the peace. It provided much needed confidence to people who no longer had faith in their own security institutions, and it created the stable, secure environment in which SSR could take place. Basic capacity and public trust in the police and military have been restored. Given the low level at which reform began, the achievement is praiseworthy (2006: 121).

At the same time, however, they conclude that the country's chronic poverty and low levels of human development suggest that SSR, if it is to be sustainable over time, must be accompanied by long-term development (Horn et al. 2006: 122).

Thus, each context has its own logics and dynamics in terms of security. While there have been instances of security sector reform and integration of former fighters into existing militaries – as in South Africa, where former African National Congress guerillas were incorporated into a newly restructured South African National Defence Force – usually SSR is carried out through the involvement of external interveners and local protagonists. The South African case has been seen as a successful endogenous process in which there was a high degree of local ownership (Gamba 2006). Often, however, the logic of external actors on SSR may not be aligned with the incentives of internal actors. For example, efforts to create a new police force in South Sudan were confronted with the reality that many of the recruits were ex-combatants of the erstwhile rebel force, now leader of government, of the Sudan People's Liberation Army (SPLA); these recruits were ill-suited to being trained as new police officers and there were concerns that the SPLA cadres were put on international police training payrolls primarily as a war-veteran benefit. The consequence has been a weak security sector in which the police are unable to perform basic functions and law enforcement falls to ill-disciplined armed forces in the SPLA, a force more suited to war-fighting than to policing; as a result, too, informal traditional leaders such as chiefs often provide security through their own paramilitary and tribal/clan forces.[13]

According to the OECD-DAC, SSR, when successful, has four principal dimensions: "establishment of effective governance, oversight, and accountability in the security system, improved delivery of security and justice services, development of local leadership and ownership of the reform process, and sustainability of justice and security service delivery" (2007: 21). Thus, the success of SSR is ultimately dependent on the establishment of a state that wields, as Weber suggests (see chapter 2), legitimate authority. Armies and security forces such as police must first have loyalty to the state, which in turn justifies their willingness to fight and be willing to sacrifice their lives for the idea of the "nation" that the state represents. One of the most critical needs, therefore, in a post-war setting is to imbue the officer corps, especially, with a common formula or ultimate mission to protect the integrity of the state.

Achieving tangible progress in security sector reform remains a challenge. This is because SSR processes are at first deeply political, and there are often human, organizational, and institutional capacity constraints in target countries. And, the breadth and length of the enterprise suggests that it is a long-term endeavor in which progress is hard to measure and, with a shift in the political winds, may be subject to reversals and collapses. Call has suggested that statebuilding objectives – to monopolize the means of violence in the state – may be at odds with peacebuilding concerns focused on preventing deadly conflict in the short term (Call 2008). Thus, in some countries non-state armed actors continue to exist alongside the official bodies of the state, and the line between what are state forces and what are the militias of various power-wielders in society is often blurred.

In Lebanon, as suggested above, the Hezbollah political party and its militia, which dominates the Shiite community as a political force and armed faction, has been named for demobilization in UNSC Resolution 1559, which also calls on Israel to withdraw from Lebanese territory; following the 2006 conflict with Israel, the Security Council again called for the disbanding of the military wing of the organization (in UNSC Resolution 1701). However, the resolution and subsequent calls for demobilization by the Council, the Secretary-General, and UN representatives on the ground (through the Office of the UN Special Coordinator, UNSCOL), have been honored in the breach. There are constant concerns in the country that sectarian conflict could erupt and shatter the newly created, neutral security force through the reformed Lebanese Internal Security Forces (ISF), a gendarmerie-type force that exists alongside the Lebanese National Army or that as an armed non-state actor it will again be engaged in cross-border war with Israel. A key issue in Lebanon, as elsewhere in fragile states, is the perception of the legitimacy of the security forces. In fragile states the competing local authorities often enjoy higher legitimacy than the state, in part because they have the capacity to provide security to communities when the state does not.

And there can be severe unintended consequences in security sector reform. In hindsight, many see the wholesale "de-Ba'athification" of Iraq following the 2003 US-led invasion and subsequent military occupation of the country as having been a colossal mistake. The belief emanating from the Pentagon during the period, and particularly from former US Secretary of Defense Donald Rumsfeld (against the advice of many in the US government), was that the experiences of statebuilding in Germany after World War II (de-Nazification) were applicable to Iraq in 2003.[14] The Coalition Provisional Authority then ordered "eliminating the party's structures and removing its leadership from positions of responsibility and authority in Iraqi society."[15]

However, given that the leaders of the military and many rank-and-file under the former dictator Saddam Hussein were principally drawn from the ranks of the Sunni population in Iraq, the decision to clean house of anyone in the military (and the state more broadly) was fatefully ill-advised. Many scholars attribute the descent of Iraq into violence in 2003 – reflecting its underlying vulnerability to conflict along both identity and economic lines – to the flawed approach to statebuilding reflected in the now notorious de-Ba'athification decision. To add insult to injury, the de-Ba'athification was overseen in large part by former Iraqi exiles ... including some extremists who were bitter enemies to many key segments of the Sunni population. Many scholars and observers also argue that the US lacked a strategic plan for rebuilding of state capacity in Iraq and that the transition plan of rapid political transformation through a brief period of constitution-making and a rapid move toward elections was a mistake of strategy and implementation with grave, long-term humanitarian and security implications.[16]

Eventually, the US reversed the ill-considered de-Ba'athification decision and decided on a broader program of reintegration and construction of a new security force in Iraq. The experience points to some of the best practices in approach and implementation in security sector reform evolved through trial and error in many settings. Although some countries have been able to manage security sector reform more or less on their own, most countries have required extensive international assistance through programs that are designed to build the capacity of the state's security forces through "equip and train" programs, the terminology now favored by the US Department of Defense.

The need to provide immediate security through international means, to (re-)construct state security institutions and to establish effective and legitimate security governance mechanisms poses a difficult challenge in post-war settings where private security actors (or non-statutory security organizations) throw into question the state authority's monopoly on the legitimate use of force. The role of non-statutory security forces in the Kosovo conflict, the proliferation of irregular forces recruiting child soldiers in Liberia and Sierra Leone, the continued authority of regional warlords in Afghanistan, the existence of a variety of local militias in Iraq, and the role of often unaccountable private military and security companies in conflict and post-war environments are good cases in point to illustrate the adverse implications of the privatization of security.

The focus on accountability for private security forces has raised anew the question of whether and how the contracting of private firms can aid (or hinder) statebuilding efforts; Deborah Avant (2009) has found that private companies can contribute to security sector reform. A key issue of whether and how the international actors of the state contract out to private military companies the provision of internal security roles, most effectively when they are overseen by international organizations who can ensure that professionalized norms and standards of accountability can be adhered to (Avant 2009). More often than not, however, reliance on private security undermines the statebuilding efforts, as Hänggi argues (2005: 8).

Community-level Security

Security in fragile states goes beyond the challenges of spoilers and contenders to legitimate state authority. Often, in post-war environments, threats to personal safety and security loom large in terms of citizen demands for better governance. Thus, there has been a shift in emphasis beyond the more traditional conceptualizations of security of armed forces to comprehensive approaches that also see security at the level of local processes and institutions. First and foremost in this pursuit of so-called human security – especially, freedom from fear – at the local level is the reform of policing.[17] Beyond policing, there is also new focus on the institutionalization of local-level conflict and dispute resolution systems that can help ameliorate local drivers of violence and can act in crisis- and conflict-prevention modes when disputes begin to escalate. In particular, such approaches reflect the evolving contextual conditions found in post-war countries, such as the prevalence of armed organizations and (often, transnational) criminal groups, terrorist networks, and gangs.

Because the police and related institutions, such as internal security forces and domestic intelligence agencies, are often the blunt edge of a repressive state, or are eviscerated in the polarization of war, a focus on post-war policing is essential. Police reform occurs in the broader context of security sector reform (as above); however, it is particularly at the level of policing where the broader theoretical notions of state–society relations are most often seen. Moreover, security at the level of communities is required for the local confidence needed to start enterprises, to take risks, and to make investments: security at the local level is a prerequisite for development. Lethal social-level violence such as murder, criminal violence, gang wars, gender-based violence, and other interpersonal violence is more extensive in those countries where police are either ill-equipped or unwilling to provide security at the community level; indeed, in some cases, police themselves are the targets of bombing, assassination, and intimidation by armed, non-state actors (Geneva Declaration Secretariat 2011: 2).

Thus, police reform and approaches such as "community policing" are at the heart of statebuilding for most citizens. For this reason, erstwhile "blue-helmeted" peacekeeping operations are increasingly being augmented by the extensive deployment of UN formed police units to augment local security when states are unable or unwilling to extend policing authority. UN peace operations with a significant police component have been seen in the 1990s and 2000s in Afghanistan, Burundi, Côte d'Ivoire, Cyprus, DRC, Georgia, Kosovo, Haiti, Liberia, Sierra Leone, Sudan, Timor-Leste, and Western Sahara. The UN police officers and units are often directly involved in the training and capacity building of local police. Additionally, UNDP has also engaged in extensive police reform programs in conflict-affected countries such as Colombia, Haiti, Kosovo, and Somalia (to name a few).

The reform of policing, like security sector reform more broadly, often takes place through in interaction of these internationally deployed police and local units. Key aims in police reform are to increase their ability to fight crime and lawlessness and, in doing so, to transform their understanding of their role in terms of protecting the rights of citizens as opposed to being the sharp end of implementation of the "coercive authority of the state." Some of the lessons learned on police reform programs aimed at extending and consolidating the authority of the state to the community level are the following.[18]

First among these findings is that no one should expect quick results in this area: the challenge of reform is not just technical – building up the "software" of human capacity through recruits, training, and mentoring, and the "hardware" of equipping the police to do their job through everything from uniforms to forensic laboratories – but it is also a matter of social trust. That is, when communities trust the police and believe that the police are not acting in a political or partisan (or, in many cases, ethnic or sectarian) way, then the police will more likely be successful. Public confidence in the police is something that may take decades, and generations, to restore in countries where police crimes and brutality were often a key grievance of communities before and during the war.

Second, reform requires that police reinterpret and reconsider their roles as agents of the state toward a human rights-based framework. These reforms mean changing mindsets as much as changing practice. For example, in countries with high rates of gender-based violence or violence against children (a problem in most conflict-affected countries, see chapter 1), retraining the police to address the problem of rape and sexual violence requires a new system and approach to relating to victims, to gathering evidence, and to subsequent protection of women who report such crimes to the police. This often means that the police will need to change the way they relate to civil society organizations such as women's groups, and indeed in programs and projects to reach out to men's populations to help educate society on human rights principles through approaches such as "street law" initiatives.

Women's security is a prerequisite to their participation in post-war recovery, and thus the focus on the linkage between police reform and women's security has become a critical policy and operational concern.[19] Jennifer Erin Salahub, in reflecting on research on women and police reform in Liberia and South Sudan, astutely argues:

> Not only do women in conflict-affected and developing countries have valuable contributions to make in terms of framing debates and interventions that affect their daily lives – contributions which often shed light on the differential impact of programs on men and women – but many of these women are also keen to participate in the security sector. This makes the police and other organizations more operationally effective in addition to helping to secure their communities and participate in the development of sustainable peace in their countries (2011: 2).

For local-level security to be effective, the direct participation by the communities is required. It is local stakeholders – civil society organizations, public health officials, religious leaders, and traditional leaders – who often understand the dynamics of conflict and who can best articulate approaches to mitigating it. Thus, community security and social cohesion approaches have emerged from organizations like UNDP and other UN entities as an approach to engagement at the local level.[20] The characteristics of such approaches is that they focus on community- and local-level dynamics that fuel violence and insecurity, they relate national-level processes such as police reform to creating the enabling environment for work at the local level, and they attempt to derive comprehensive approaches to the problems through coordinating them across traditional development programming interventions.

The approach has been used in contexts such as Bosnia, Burundi, Kosovo, El Salvador, Nepal, and Sierra Leone, and pair interventions such as small arms and light weapons control to community-based policing techniques, access to justice through alternative dispute resolution mechanisms, and the development of local-level security plans. As well, there is a focus on addressing the root causes of violence at the local level in terms of creating new peace architectures, or dialogue and crisis-response mechanisms that allow opportunities for dialogue among key stakeholders (such as the police, community leaders, religious leaders, and conflict protagonists), early warning, and crisis response. Such initiatives often feature the formation of national, regional, and local-level peace committees – an approach pioneered in South Africa to manage transition-related violence.[21]

Conclusion

Achieving security in war-torn societies, to be successful, must ultimately get at the heart of the disaffection, alienation, and desperation that often leads to participation in insurgencies and criminal organizations and, through frustration, to anti-social violence. Thus, community security and security reform more broadly cannot be delinked from the problems of continued acute poverty and unemployment. In the short term, programs targeted at the economic reintegration and livelihoods of former ex-combatants are critical, as are rapid employment schemes for at-risk youth and programs designed to rehabilitate former gang members. In the long term, however, the answers to insecurity are often found in the quest to address the deep economic drivers of predatory politics, corruption and rent-seeking, and in reduction of chronic poverty after war.

CHAPTER FIVE

Capacity: Creating the Conditions for Development

The inability of governments to deliver the basic conditions and services needed for socio-economic development directly contributes to societal-level fragility in states confronted with chronic poverty: when the state is absent and fails to address basic human needs, social groups may be mobilized to protest, rebel, and to wage revolution. Thus it is through improved state capacities to deliver these conditions (such as the rule of law) and services (such as universal primary education) that the root causes of economic deprivation and social tension can be addressed through a new approach and content to development policies. From ensuring the accountability of the state – combating corruption – to the practical aspects of taxes for basic services such as water, health care, and education, the relationship between state capacity and long-term development is critical.

Corruption undermines the legitimacy of the state and can generate new grievances. Perhaps no case is more exemplary than Afghanistan, which during the period in which it was the world's number one aid recipient, corruption increased throughout society, together with black-market trading, drug running, and arms trafficking ... nearly $12 billion dollars annually during the height of statebuilding efforts.[1] Anti-corruption efforts such as the "National Priority Program on Transparency and Accountability," have been at best feeble, and have not won the full support of the Karzai government. Without a viable state that can prevent and punish corruption through the rule of law, which can keep ruling elites accountable through separation of powers, and which can deliver basic or core public services to the people, development is impossible. And, conversely, without improvements in education, health care, and livelihoods in society, the state itself is unlikely to enjoy much legitimacy as an expected provider of such public goods.

This chapter explores the role of the state in facilitating development in post-war countries. First, it explores the political economy of post-war statebuilding in terms of wartime patterns that leave distortion and disabilities and which inform the starting points for considering post-war economic recovery. Countries that are highly dependent on natural resources – either extractive industries, or primary commodity agricultural exports – are not only vulnerable to conflict to begin with (see chapter 1), but they also present special difficulties of natural resource wealth sharing and transformative processes like privatization in the post-war period. Because many fragile states experience chronic poverty, the chapter then looks at the experience of poverty reduction strategies in the post-war period and the lessons learned on enabling economic recovery, particularly for basic livelihoods. Often, in divided societies such as Guatemala, Nepal, or South Africa, where inequalities were a strong driver of war and which persist into the post-war period, the economic agenda after war is often about radical social re-engineering to remediate the horizontal inequalities that characterize these stratified societies. A landmark 2008 UNDP report on post-war economics argued that getting development right is a key pillar of the statebuilding approach.

> Sustainable economic recovery is . . . essential to address the underlying risks in the post-conflict period of renewed conflict, especially from the lethal combination of high levels of poverty, unemployment, and hopelessness. A strong and

inclusive state is essential for securing stability and recovery. Post-conflict countries need to rebuild state capacity quickly, including the capacity to collect revenue and to allocate it effectively. Improved transparency is especially important in natural-resource rich countries where there is much potential for rent-seeking (UNDP 2008: xxiii).

From this perspective, development and security agendas are one and the same in such contexts: that security is needed for development, and development is needed for security – while cliché – is a broadly understood premise in the statebuilding debates. The key to post-war economic recovery is the reform and evolution of governance capacities to formulate national development strategies, to bridge capacity gaps in public administration with outside help, to extend government services to the people at the local level, and to create the macroeconomic and microeconomic structures and incentives that foster development. At the same time, there is a risk in merging development and security agendas. Efforts by the US government to use so-called Provincial Reconstruction Teams (PRTs) in Iraq and Afghanistan to foster local-level development as part of a broader counter-insurgency strategy were criticized for jeopardizing aid through its politicization, such that the PRTs suffer from a "clash of mindsets."[2] In a similar vein, efforts to integrate humanitarian assistance into broader UN strategies for peace and development in post-war countries have seen criticism for jeopardizing the neutrality of humanitarian actors, especially in the DRC where the UN has been called in to facilitate statebuilding through a robust military engagement against armed spoilers.[3]

The chapter explores a key question: What works in terms of building the capacity of the state, especially the key elements that are prerequisites for development: stable institutions, revenue raising, a professionalized civil service, strengthened local governance institutions, and improvements in the capacities of the historically disadvantaged segments of society to participate in public policy formulation and implementation?

The Political Economy of Post-war Statebuilding

In considering how economic patterns affect the extent to which post-war countries can regain, or gain anew, capacities to facilitate development requires a look at several key factors. First, each context has its own path dependency, and orthodox economic theories applied without consideration of the local dynamics of economic activity can cause more harm than good. Secondly, the political economy perspective requires an understanding of various levels of analysis: from global trade, aid, and foreign direct investment flows to the individual level of understanding incentives and economic behavior, including the incentives of ruling elites. The key aim of post-war economic recovery is not just to recreate prior patterns of exploitation and injustice (which have often led to conflict in the first place), but to re-orient the state "differently and better" according to the UNDP . . . toward a developmental state (UNDP 2008: 5). Some, such as Mick Moore and James Putzel, have accurately described the developmental state as one that is explicitly "pro-poor" or oriented toward addressing the plight of the many who live in chronic poverty. In their insightful view, what are needed are states that can create and shape opportunities for the poor (Moore and Putzel 1999).

Macroeconomic factors are determined in broad historical patterns over the course of a conflict. In Sudan, for example the discovery and exploitation of oil in southern Sudan was a driver of initial re-escalation of the civil war in the mid-1980s. Oil revenues contributed to the capacity of the state and rebel factions to wage the war for the duration of the conflict, and the prospect of sharing oil revenues through cooperative exploitation was a factor in negotiating the 2005 Comprehensive Peace Agreement (CPA). Indeed, oil wealth was shared, albeit not to the letter of the agreement (the Government of Sudan allegedly failed to transfer the share allotted to the new Government of South Sudan), through the interim period of the Sudanese CPA and now into the post-independence period. However, the Sudanese case underscores the continued role that oil and money play in the conflict: continued violence in disputed areas such as Abyei between Sudan and now independent South Sudan is spurred by unresolved territorial claims to oil-rich regions (Shankleman 2011).

Thus, in some contexts, the state is used in a post-war setting to create institutions that can manage economic structures that run deep in society, such as patterns of land ownership, or that directly affect conflict dynamics, such as the question of extractive industry concessions for oil, gas, or mineral deposits. In South Africa, after the apartheid-era conflict ended in the mid-1990s, the African National Congress inherited a fairly high-capacity state and made a strategic decision to build on the current state structures – however illegitimate they may have been during white-minority rule – rather than cleaning house and starting from scratch. In contrast, at the end of the Liberian war in 2003, government buildings were wrecked and looted, local government ceased to function, public servants had scattered around the region and world, and taxation and spending by the state more or less ceased to exist.

Because path dependency matters so much, it is helpful to differentiate contexts of post-war economic recovery by development type, much like the political starting points for statebuilding in terms of war-termination outcomes. First, there are, according to Graham Brown, Langer Arnim, and Frances Stewart, three categories of states in terms of their economic or development starting points: countries with chronic poverty and lack of economic opportunities, with very low or negligible incomes, such as Afghanistan, Haiti, or Sierra Leone; countries with considerable high-value natural resources, such as Angola, Iraq, or South Sudan; and countries with high horizontal inequalities across identity lines, such as Guatemala or Sri Lanka (2007: 3). They point out, as does Christopher Cramer (2009), that while most economies decline during war, in many contexts wartime economies actually grow, albeit in malicious ways in which certain factions or groups accumulate wealth through capture of key natural resource supply chains, control of markets (for example, of needed medicines, fuel, or appliances such as generators), or control of export-derived revenue. During the war in Liberia, the NGO Global Witness alleged that former Liberia President Charles Taylor had assets of $150–210 million in 2003 from timber exports, diamond smuggling, and mining concessions; he used some of the revenue from the far-flung enterprises to buy arms to fuel the war despite a UN arms embargo.[4]

The economic effects of civil war are typically devastating. Capital flight has typically drained the country of money for reinvestment, and in the course of conflict illicit and parallel economies that are controlled by warlords and networks of criminal enterprises can undermine confidence further. Post-war countries experience endemic economic problems, including high levels of unemployment, high dependency ratios (the number of people depending on a single income), inflation and low savings rates, and high prices for basic commodities, especially food, medicines, and energy. Governments may face deep fiscal deficits (often from wartime spending), high levels of domestic and international debt, and the basic inability to raise tax revenue locally. Comparative research on these poorest countries identifies six distinct economic factors that are associated with the risk of conflict recurrence: income insecurity, weak economic growth, persistent socio-economic horizontal inequalities, dependence on abundant natural resources, high unemployment, and poor economic governance (Collier et al. 2008).

Equally, because inequality along group lines is often a strong driver of conflict, policies to address the needs of historically disadvantaged communities are central to building a state that is based on the law and the ability of people to have security in their ownership or access to land and livelihoods. In El Salvador and South Africa, a key aspect of statebuilding has been the creation of land reform institutions and processes and the redistribution of ownership rights through a legal process of land-tenure reform. In Nepal, the question of statebuilding has much to do with rebuilding the legitimacy of the state at the local level, where it was perceived to reinforce a feudal system of entrenched inequality (Gates and Murshed 2005).

Moreover, as the example of Nepal's Terai region illustrates, statebuilding will also involve equipping the new administrators and structures to address the underlying problems of endemic poverty that have given rise not only to armed rebellion against the state by the Maoists, but also the criminalization of society and deep vulnerabilities of youth to recruitment into armed gangs.[5] It is in these types of mal- or un-governed regions where there are the greatest vulnerabilities for human trafficking and vulnerability of women and girls into slavery or all youth into forced labor.[6] Thus, statebuilding in Nepal – as it has in El Salvador and South Africa – will require remediation of historical horizontal inequalities. This means specific and deliberate policies designed to address historical and deeply embedded social structures.

The depth of the economic challenges that face the most impoverished of the fragile states suggests a cautious approach to macroeconomic reform; in many cases, people have developed survival strategies during the conflict and it is critical not to make things worse by importing radical economic change models that may well entail deep social costs to the poorest in society (such as removal of subsidies). The World Bank's landmark *World Development Report 2011* emphasizes jobs, security, and the rule of law as the key macroeconomic factors related to recovery in fragile states. In the view of many, at the heart of restoring government-led economic functions is a focus on the monetary policy and capacity of the state, to arrest hyper-inflation, curb the most corrupt abuses of power, and to stabilize currency exchange rates (Ghani and Lockhart 2008). These factors are critical in post-war settings to restore and to stabilize trade flows and to garner foreign exchange earnings.

Paradoxes of Plenty

Also critical in the early phases of recovery is the capacity of the government to be able to negotiate, oversee, and regulate foreign direct investment (FDI), particularly in those sectors that were at the heart of conflict dynamics such as the extractive industries.[7] In countries emerging from war, development is equally linked to core issues of conflict management, particular in the case of conflicts driven by natural resources. Post-war countries are often described as suffering from the "paradox of plenty." With the recognition that natural resources form a key source of revenue during war (which increases war duration) and in funding spoilers in the post-war environment, there are new efforts to develop mechanisms to link global monitoring and transparency rules with local capacities to implement them. These include, for example, efforts to create new programs such as natural resource wealth-sharing schemes – such as the Kimberly Process and the concomitant Diamond-Area Community Development Fund in Sierra Leone – that not only limit access to resources to fund conflict through control regimes, but that also create new incentives for local peace through the sharing of natural resource wealth.

Global governance regimes, such as the Kimberley Process or the Extractive Industries Transparency Initiative (EITI), in which countries and companies participate, provide institutionalization of mechanisms for transparency, accountability, and the control of corruption. These global–local models are at the forefront of governance innovations designed to get at the critical transnational factors in state capture and corruption in the poorest conflict-affected countries. The EITI, for example, is a system of set global standards for industries such as oil and gas and mining of precious metals that is based on a global governance coalition model, in which governments, companies, and civil society participate. At the end of 2011, some 29 countries were participating in the EITI regime as implementing countries, which obligates mutual transparency from companies, which are required to publish what they pay for exploration or extraction projects; in turn governments are required to publish what they receive. World Bank officials tout the EITI as an innovative mechanism to remedy the natural resource curse, the paradox by which countries with extensive natural resources experience dire poverty and resource-related conflicts (Caspary 2012).

For example, the continued instability and insurgent violence that has seen mass atrocities in eastern DRC, including mass rapes and crimes against humanity, are fueled in part by capture of the source or supply chain routes from the region into the global commodities markets. Many of the minerals from eastern DRC are essential elements in new technologies including mobile phones, particularly tin, tantalum (aka coltan), tungsten, and gold. The non-government Enough!

Project estimated that rebel forces or armed criminal groups often control the mines, extort money from transporters and other key points in the supply chain (such as border crossings), and often use the revenues (an estimated $185 million in 2008 alone) to pay recruits, buy arms, control territory, and prey on the local population (Enough! 2009).

The Democratic Republic of Congo's participation in the EITI as an implementing country seems to be a test case as to whether global–local processes such as these can create the external agencies of restraint needed for good domestic governance where it matters most in terms of the flow of foreign exchange earnings to the state. The DRC example and the experiences of the EITI more broadly suggest that best practices in managing the resource curse in post-conflict countries is joining up global governance with efforts to build the capacity of national states in areas such as security sector reform and the capacity of local and national authorities to participate in global regimes. This is true not only in terms of extractive industries, but also in areas of illicit markets where transitioning states need to be able to participate in global anti-transnational crime efforts, for example through the United Nations Office of Drugs and Crime (UNODC).

The look at extraction as a source of revenue raising implies that it is necessary to find alternative ways for fragile states to mobilize revenues through taxation beyond the primary commodities trade or through illicit means. Indeed, weak domestic revenue raising and dependency on international aid flows has underlined accountability between the citizens and the state, with government officials often more beholden to donors for their resource flows than to their own people. An OECD-DAC study found that many fragile states – Afghanistan, Zimbabwe, Haiti, Timor-Leste, the Central African Republic, and Sierra Leone – all raise less than 12 percent of government revenues through taxation; and those that raise more than 45 percent of their own resources – Angola, Congo-Brazzaville, and Iraq – are all dependent on oil exports.[8] Thus, improving government capacities for effective tax collection has been seen as a critical priority for donors. Some suggest that even a little tax-levying capacity is useful in symbolically linking state and society, notwithstanding the reality that many fragile states will be aid-dependent for years to come.[9]

Thus, control of natural resources and the prevention of their exploitation by armed non-state actors, whether rebel factions or criminal enterprises, are essential to the statebuilding enterprise. So, too, are efforts to integrate into the national development policies of states comprehensive approaches to wealth-sharing. In countries such as Iraq with high endowments of oil and gas, but which are regionally concentrated (often along ethnic fault lines, in this case between predominantly Sunni and Kurdish regions of the country), the negotiation of comprehensive wealth-sharing agreements is an approach designed to address the incentives for territorial fracturing along identity lines and indeed secessionist tendencies. In Iraq, the failed effort in 2007 to negotiate a hydrocarbon law is indicative of the difficulty of reaching comprehensive wealth-sharing agreements, as well as their ultimate implementation. Without external regimes such as the EITI to monitor and verify revenue and distribution of wealth, often even the best-conceived wealth-sharing agreements are insufficient to enable the state to operate effectively as a re-distributor of natural resource revenues.

Addressing Chronic Poverty and Acute Deprivation

As discussed in chapter 1, conflict and poverty are deeply related, particular in cases where there is deep and persistent inequality, where large sections of the population live in conditions of chronic poverty and acute deprivation, and especially where depravity and the inability to create a livelihood overlaps with long-standing, and socially constructed, ethnic identities.[10] These conditions are exacerbated by the total or near absence of the state in providing basic social services that today form party of the state's collective obligation to ensure not only freedom from fear, but also freedom from want, as the two pillars of human security. In the worst instances, where such endemic conditions of poverty lead to humanitarian emergencies, the core of basic functions of government in providing public goods to alleviate poverty – clean water and sanitation, health care, and education – are substituted by international humanitarian providers.

Thus, a critical factor in statebuilding is the creation anew of national development strategies and planning, of reform of the public administration to have incentives and to have the institutional, organizational, and human capacities and skills to provide services, and the actual provision of these services particularly by local governments where the state and citizenry most closely meet. Additionally, there is concern not only with access to services such as education, but also their consistency and quality. One of the most critical considerations for the recovery of state capacities after war is how to restore the legitimacy of the state as a service provider (OECD-DAC 2010b).

The restoration of the core functions of the state cannot be done without attention to the challenge of restoring state–society relations. During conflict, people naturally adopt survival strategies, and local informal institutions – from civil society to religious leaders and traditional authorities – step into the void created by weak state capacity to deliver services. In many of the most impoverished societies, the state never really provided these services to begin with. Thus, the arena of restoring service delivery by the state – and of creating revenue streams through taxation that recreate a "tax-mediated" social contract – often means seeking to disable informal systems that already provide essential services.

For this reason, as in many other areas of statebuilding, there are dilemmas for international aid providers and for governments alike as to how to re-establish the state's role as a provider of essential services. In the short term, delivering services through these informal institutions may be needed, but over time there needs to be gradual shift toward enhancing the legitimacy of the state as a provider of these essentials for long-term development. This is true in part because informal institutions such as traditional leaders may not be accountable to society as a whole, and access to the services may be limited for the entire population. In places like Iraq, there are very direct relationships between security-oriented objectives and the acquiescence of local populations, such as those of the counter-insurgency programs, in which the US military pioneered the development of Provincial Reconstruction Teams as a "hearts and minds" strategy. In the DRC, the UN has struggled with its humanitarian and service-delivery provision (especially in emergency health care), and the peace enforcement mission against the rebel forces of the Democratic Forces for the Liberation of Rwanda (FLDR), which is explicitly related to a long-term strategy of statebuilding, is perhaps the least likely case of success.

There are practical implementation problems as well. For example, short-term measures may involve the provision of cash payments to beneficiaries as a tool of post-war stabilization in an effort to provide for basic livelihoods that reduce the vulnerabilities of youth, especially to recruitment into militias, rebel forces, or criminal gangs. For example, in Iraq, cash payments were provided for (nominal) work to thousands of young Shiites in Basra as a way to reduce their desperation and the appeal of militia groups like the Sadrists that had challenged the post-2003 intervention efforts to recreate the Iraqi state. The program, funded by donors such as the European Commission and the governments of Japan, Belgium, and the UK, among others, provided emergency employment for projects such as infrastructure improvements and other labor-intensive work. Administered by UNDP, the nearly $42 million program was explicitly designed to give the formerly disadvantaged Shiite youth a sense of hope and aspirations for the future in building the country amidst the ongoing violence that accompanied the post-Saddam transition.[11]

Similar to this are short-term measures that are designed to rapidly build the capacity of states emerging from civil war through the deployment of skilled professionals who have been in the Diaspora during the conflict. In Liberia, in an effort to kick-start the state's public administration capacities, international donors funded the return of educated and skilled Liberians to the country to take up posts as program directors, technical advisors in ministries, and local administrators. The program in Liberia, like similar programs elsewhere (such as Haiti, Palestine, South Sudan, and Timor-Leste), address the short-term challenges of capacity deficits in key areas of governance (particularly, for example, financial management of local government administration), but at a price: often those who fled the country or who have lived outside during times of conflict – and often, who were politically active from afar – may not be well accepted by local communities when they return. Thus, the use of diaspora communities in quick restoration of state capacities is inherently problematic as a human resource solution, even though gains have been made in implementing such programs more effectively (Brinkerhoff 2009, 2010).

Because of the vexatious nature of either international, local non-governmental, or diaspora-community capacity substitution to provide effective service delivery, the key to post-war development is one of finding the local, indigenous drivers of economic recovery and growth. In essence, this requires looking at how the state can provide the broader enabling environment for stability to allow for local markets, sustainable agricultural livelihoods, and new forms of services (such as selling sharing of mobile phone credit). Because many fragile countries also experience high vulnerability to natural disaster, as in the devastating and recurrent earthquakes and flooding in Pakistan, countries that have experienced conflict need very well-considered environmental programs and disaster-risk reduction to restore health ecosystems.[12] In this area, a critical need is to address those governance capacities that are most needed to address complex problems such as environmental restoration, the effects of climate change, and intermediate pressures from environmental effects such as increased internal and trans-boundary migration. This means that statebuilding will increasingly require building the capacities of public administrators not just to "make" policy, but to have the skills and personality to be able to design, convene, and participate with local communities in development processes to reconcile competing interests brought on by such changes.

Governance is evolving from a top-down authoritative set of decision-makers to a view of the developmental state that is more about inclusion and participation. Indeed, in many of the most important issue areas, such as global environment, education, and health, as well as in governance best practices, there is increasingly the evolution of global public policy networks that seek to integrate states into the most up-to-date knowledge, processes, and methods for delivering services. But a missing link in these networks is frequently the lack or weakness of local capacities in government partners. Weber was right: statebuilding and public administration reform are critical for the state to have much developmental capacity. Public administration reform from the bottom up and the top down is perhaps one of the most difficult, yet one of the most urgent, tasks in post-war statebuilding.

Fortunately, the UN and others have already begun to devote substantial attention to best practices in public administration reform and the practical ways in which the organization and sympathetic donors can contribute to developing a long-term strategy of rebuilding the nuts and bolts of the state at national, regional, and local levels.[13] First, at the national level, there is a critical need to stabilize economic policy making and to have a long-term agenda. In Liberia, for example, with the facilitation of the UN and the ownership of the government of Ellen Johnson Sirleaf, the country has adopted a reasonable yet still ambitious ten-year strategy to build the capacity of the state to deliver essential services.[14] This approach, combined with efforts to improve citizen monitoring of the country's Poverty Reduction Strategy, appears critical to building a responsive state in post-war Liberia.

Where there are challenges (as in police reform; see chapter 4), the long-term plans often fall by the wayside in the messy and difficult realities of working with ministries that may be prone to corruption or a culture of ineptness, where the networks among local actors are unclear, or where ministries may be "captured" by an ethnic or identity group. These challenges have been seen in countries such as Kosovo, Iraq, Lebanon, Liberia, and South Sudan, such that the development aid community has already sought to understand the principles of a "do-no-harm" approach to statebuilding (see chapter 7). When enabling ministries and empowering local officials, there is the real possibility that efforts to create a meritocratic, Weberian state based on rational service delivery may well run aground in the complex local political economies, in which distribution is based more on patronage and identity networks than any sense of loyalty to the poorest populations that need most direct government assistance.

The idea of a development-oriented state requires a new kind of approach to deliver services in two critical and related areas that underpin development in fragile and non-fragile situations alike: education and health care. Fragile and conflict-affected countries face a variety of education system challenges, from primary and secondary education to vocational and the often weak or disabled higher education system.[15] In particular, core capacities are needed to develop a strategy for financing of education and a political settlement in which there is a dedication of key elites to a restored education policy. Save the Children, an international non-governmental organization (INGO), reports that the money spent on a child's education in the most developed countries is more than 500 times that spent in the bottom third of least developed countries that are beset by conflict.[16] At the primary level, a priority is the pursuit of the MDG targets on education in the poorest circumstances, taking into account the particular needs of especially vulnerable children, for example those who are displaced by conflict. At secondary level, it is quite clear that a critical long-term conflict-prevention target is to increase both male and female secondary school enrollment. When males drop out, they are especially vulnerable to recruitment into armed groups. For girls and young women, access to education is the essential ingredient of a lifetime in which there is the possibility to be free of discrimination and discriminatory violence and to enjoy equally the grandiose promises of international resolutions as enshrined in the Convention on the Elimination of Discrimination Against Women and reflected in UNSC Resolution 1325 on the promotion of women's participation in peacebuilding.

Indeed, today it is well understood that development gains are made when the fundamental human rights, choices, and participation of women increases.[17] Countries that can use the window of opportunity in the post-war period to rewrite the rules of the game regarding the roles of women are more likely to see development, and arguably to see peace as well (Hudson et al. 2009). Certainly this belief is behind the Nobel Peace Prize awarded in 2011 to Liberian President Ellen Johnson Sirleaf and Leymah Gbowee (together with democracy campaigner Tawakul Karman of Yemen); in announcing the 2011 award, the Norwegian Nobel Committee asserted that "We cannot achieve democracy and lasting peace in the world unless women obtain the same opportunities as men to influence developments at all levels of society."[18] Women's security and rights have been seen as essential key areas of human security to include food security, protection of children, environmental protection, and reproductive health.

How societies treat women and girls is in fact a key indicator of whether the state is one in which security exists for society as a whole, both in terms of the slide into civil war but also in terms of whether that state is involved in international warfare. In engaging if not sometimes controversial research, Valerie Hudson and her colleagues have presented a compelling, evidenced-based case; they report:

> We find a strong and significant relationship between the physical security of women and the peacefulness of states. Furthermore, we believe there are sound theoretical reasons to expect this relationship to obtain: when evolutionary forces predisposing to violent patriarchy are not checked through the use of cultural selection and social learning to ameliorate gender inequality, we assert that dysfunctional templates of violence and control diffuse throughout society and are manifested in state security and behavior (Hudson et al. 2009: 42).

This and other research is beginning to confirm a core tenet of a liberal approach to statebuilding, that there is a clear, direct relationship between the physical security of women, women's participation in development, and the relative peacefulness of the state and society as a whole. Certainly, these days, there is already wide consensus at all levels of the UN in its experience in post-war countries that women's rights are essential to the long-term development of both security and development, and they are integral to any advanced-thinking theory of statebuilding into the twenty-first century.[19] According the UN Department of Economic and Social Affairs (DESA),

> Gender equality in the distribution of economic and financial resources has positive multiplier effects for a range of key development goals, including poverty reduction and the welfare of children. Both micro-level efficiency results through increased household productivity and macro-efficiency results through positive synergies between indicators of gender equality and economic growth have been recorded.[20]

Conclusion

What are the ingredients for long-term success in building the capacity of the state to deliver development, and in doing so strengthen its own legitimacy? Clearly, there are no silver bullets. For some countries, such as the Côte d'Ivoire and its cocoa, DRC and its diamonds and coltan, or Sudan and South Sudan with their oil, development policy is not only a problem of resources for building the state, but of conflicts over the distribution of revenues to or through the state. In other environments, war has left no real state to speak of: in Liberia in 1997–2003 or in Timor-Leste in 2000, conflict has resulted in armed actors essentially destroying or expelling the state (respectively), and thus building state capacity for development is a problem of thinking not from above, but from the ground up.

This means that statebuilding for development in post-war countries will require rethinking orthodoxy and over-generalized approaches. The World Bank's 2011 *World Development*

Report on recovery from conflict and fragility did a good job of relating to the best work of many economists and from some honest soul-searching by practitioners about the principal conditions for post-war economic recovery in countries suffering from conflict. The multi-million dollar report's principal conclusion makes sense: to focus on security, jobs, and a stable environment through governance and particularly public administration reforms to include the judiciary (World Bank 2011).

Ultimately, however, the 2011 *World Development Report*'s view on statebuilding seems strangely incomplete. Despite all the well-meaning effort and the depth of research that lurks behind the WDR 2011, the world's premier development organization has produced a hoped-for landmark study that has a curious and rather large blind spot for what also matters much in post-war countries: that people are free from oppression by corrupt, captured states that serve more the interests of a particular group of elites or of a particular identity and neglect the needs of those who struggle to survive. No less than anywhere else, and perhaps more so, publics in countries emerging from civil war want democracy and human rights. The WDR 2011, sadly, does not focus on democracy at all and mentions elections in passing and only in reference to the case of Ghana. This is regrettable when we know that statebuilding elites in countries such as Afghanistan, Burundi, Iraq, or Zimbabwe will fiercely contest state power in the electoral arena. In sum, the legitimacy of the state in the twenty-first century rests not just on economic performance and "delivering the goods," but equally on democratic participation.

CHAPTER SIX

Legitimacy: Toward a Democratic State

The recent transitions in the Middle East suggest that the post-Cold War tidal wave of transitions from authoritarian or war-torn countries to democracy is not yet over. Democratization, as these transitions have poignantly shown, can be conflict-inducing, and in the worst instances can degenerate into civil war when maniacal elites cling to power and turn the coercive force of the state against their own people. Indeed, some of the Arab Spring states such as Libya and Syria descended into violence that breaches the limit to becoming atrocities against humanity, rightly gaining the attention of the International Criminal Court. In these cases, the authority of the state was grotesquely targeted against unarmed civilians – society – invoking from international observers recognition that the state has failed in its core responsibility to protect citizens . . . from itself (see chapter 1).

While the Libyan civil war was brief compared to many of the longer imbroglios of the 1980s and 1990s that initially spawned the focus on statebuilding, the experience there reinforces that in the twenty-first century, from the Libya context to the most difficult cases of Afghanistan, the DRC, Iraq, or Somalia, the logic of exit from civil war must relate to the ways in which the state provides for and indeed interacts with its own society. In most instances, war-to-democracy transitions characterize the third dimensions of statebuilding into the twenty-first century (Jarstad and Sisk 2008). Countries emerging from war are also going through turbulent and often violent democratic transitions, and actors are perplexed over difficult questions like transitional justice, writing a new constitution, and contesting for power through uncertain, ill-administered, and often violence-ridden electoral processes.

While many argue that democracy should be deferred for a decade or more in post-war environments while the institutions of the state are built first, this view is practically unrealistic in the contemporary age. Any account of the statebuilding concept and practice into the twenty-first century must in fact grapple with the key questions of how the state can be held accountable. Accountability is essential to statebuilding in terms of the division of power among state institutions, but more importantly in how citizens can hold those in government accountable, how civil society can participate, and how basic yet uniformly problematic institutions like parliament can perform better in response to the international obligation[1] that states must govern *democratically*. Difficult issues, not least among them how to develop a coherent and stable party system that transcends deep divisions of identity, stand in the way of a smooth path to democratization. Moreover, fragile states are deeply vulnerable to new interrelated crises, such as impasse in the formation of governments, election-related violence, and leadership successions. Yet democracy cannot be deferred because interim governments are inevitably weak and lack sufficient legitimacy to rule (Gutierri and Piombo 2007).

As well, powerful countries in the international system see the promotion of democracy as essential to their national interest as a strategic approach to statebuilding, emanating from the basic premise that democratic states are more likely to see development, and be peaceful, both internationally and in terms of their internal processes of conflict management (Doyle 1983). There is an international democracy-building global network that provides assistance in the key areas of citizenship law, registration of voters, regulation of political parties, and election security, to name just a few. However, the track record of democracy promotion after conflict is notably mixed, and in some cases (such as following the Cambodian elections of 1993), the international community may inadvertently facilitate a process of democratic transition that instead leads to the capture of the state by a single political party.[2] Thus, election events are pathways for the acquisition of state power that can lead to conflict and capture. For this reason, the democratization agenda as a whole has been under attack on the sequence, timing, and logic of post-war elections.

This chapter addresses the core dilemmas of statebuilding as applied to the political dimensions of democracy. The theme of the chapter is that democracy must go beyond the so-called fallacy of electoralism. Elections matter, especially to those who contest them. For this reason, it is also a myth that the international community is responsible for foisting elections on countries after war (with the possible exceptions of Afghanistan and Iraq, although some argue that the formerly voiceless in these societies were in fact yearning for democratic voice). But democracy is more than an occasional cast of a ballot, and democracy-building efforts by outsiders must be much more attuned to local dynamics and much more focused on principles of inclusion and actual participation of civil society and informal authorities in decision making.

Moreover, democracy is about restraining the state, and creating institutions through which it can be held accountable (Schedler 1999). Throughout the chapter, I argue that democracy is about the accountability of the state to its people. We evaluate horizontal accountability, or the ways in which different centers of power within the state can hold each other accountable (particularly the ability of independent anti-corruption institutions), and "vertical" accountability, or how the people can hold their leaders to account. And we consider new developments in "social accountability," or the ways in which civil society, public interest groups, and ordinary citizens can hold the state accountable through direct participation in the service delivery aspects of governance, for example through crowd sourcing or "citizen score cards." The chapter concludes with the view that new approaches to democracy building are urgently needed that prioritize inclusivity and that re-structure the rules of the game for elites toward facilitating a participatory state. Democratization as a project must be more focused on institutions that provide incentives for cooperation, consensus, and participation over those that create a fight-to-the-death competition, through the ballot box, for the "prize" of state power.

Debating Democratization after War

Democratization after war can be deeply destabilizing. The movement toward democracy entails changes and shifts of power, and it raises fears in the incumbents for their personal future, opening up visions of aggrandizement by opposition elites who have battled the regime for their cause. The sheer uncertainty of transitional moments increases the risk of use of violence by those who lose or fear losing power and by those that feel that they should gain more. Introducing democracy in the wake of civil war raises a stark question: How can societies, shattered by war, with all the deep social enmity, personal suffering, and economic devastation that war brings, simultaneously move toward peace *and* democracy when competitive politics and hard-fought elections exacerbate social and political conflict?[3]

This reality has raised deep questions about the utility of democratization approaches in the wake of conflict. While many of the initial successes in the post-Cold War period of reasonably successful transition from war to peace, such as in Namibia, El Salvador, and Mozambique, were based on an essentially democratizing model of change, this model ran aground in the messy realities of cases such as Angola, where early elections (in 1992) led to renewed war, or in Burundi in 1993 where elections were a catalyst for renewed genocidal violence. Similarly, a rush to elections in Bosnia in 1996 arguably set the stage for the ossification of the political system along ethnic lines over which the war was fought, and no amount of post-1995 election efforts to reform the system to break down ethno-nationalist control of politics has been successful since (Belloni 2007, Bieber 2006, Bose 2002, Chandler 2006, Weller and Wolff 2007).

The example of Bosnia as well as the ill-considered electoral process in Iraq in 2005 and troubled first-round Afghanistan elections in 2004 (presidential) and 2005 (parliamentary), have raised critical questions about whether the liberal peacebuilding framework (Newman 2009), essentially drawn from earlier models of transitional change from the experience of the third wave of democratization that began in 1974 with Portugal's Revolution of the Carnations, is applicable in postwar contexts (Bermeo 2003).

Moreover, critics assert that often the preconditions for successful democratization – particularly security sector reform and economic reform measures to "break the conflict trap" – are usually absent.[4] Civil society is weak and often divided, and key institutions like the security forces or police serve the interests of political factions and not the state or the people. Finally, there are real practical concerns that in post-war contexts there are typically large numbers of internally displaced persons and refugees, and wartime migration has led to a redistribution of the population making practical needs like boundary delimitation (drawing of electoral boundaries) politically and practically vexatious.

While liberal peacebuilding critique is good at pointing out the palpable problems of post-war democratization, it offers little guidance on a "statebuilding first" perspective. Indeed, it tends to ignore the basic reality that protagonists in conflict themselves, such as the anti-apartheid movement in South Africa or the Maoists in Nepal, fight for democracy and are unwilling to defer the electoral moment until either violence subsides or until state transformation is complete. As Kristine Höglund (2008) has artfully shown, often violence does not subside and it is not possible to begin the statebuilding enterprise until electoral processes yield a new legitimacy for the state. As a result, while there may be intellectual appeal for an approach that argues for statebuilding before liberalization and democratization, in the twenty-first century it is unlikely that any post-war regime can rule long without the stamp of legitimacy approval that comes from the ballot box.

Conceptually and practically, there is a solid foundation for democratization as the long-term route to peace. In the cold reality of negotiated peace agreements following civil war today, where the international community's normative and material levers of inducement are ubiquitously brought to bear, the war-termination choice for a process of democratization is a compelling choice for several reasons for protagonists and the international community alike. For protagonists, democratization becomes an exit pathway from civil war, and it is not by accident that wars ending in negotiated settlements set up a democratization pathway as an exit strategy to costly armed conflict and mutually hurting stalemates. For the international community, and particularly for UN agencies bound by the organization's normative commitments to democracy and human rights, endorsing a peacebuilding or statebuilding plan that is non-democratic is simply not an option. Thus, while the critiques of the liberal peace (see chapter 2) can deconstruct the problem and call for a statebuilding-first perspective, they are often out of step with both the logic of protagonists as they exit civil war and the real normative constraints that guide international action.

The search for institutional solutions to resolve these dilemmas of democratization has focused on ways to restrict the competitive nature of democracy (what theorist Robert Dahl has termed "contestation"[5]), while maintaining the core focus on participation. As a result, there is increasing focus on middle-ground, sequenced approaches to democratization in post-war countries. Unlike the case of Bosnia, where the constitution of the country was hammered out in a short period of time with the intense pressures of mediation by a great powers using their coercive, external authority (Holbrooke 1999), the most attractive models of change today combine a period of rule by elected authorities on an interim basis, which then serve at the same time as a constitutional assembly. This sequence of change, seen in prior cases such as South Africa and more recent ones like Nepal and now in Libya, pair democratization elements such as an initial election (1994 in South Africa; 2008 in Nepal; 2012 in Libya) with a process for writing a new constitution.

As the eminent Italian scholar Giovanni Sartori has argued, constitutions and the rules of the game they reflect can be written in such a way as to engineer or build in certain outcomes through the design of the structure of political institutions (1968). Institutions are but systems of rules that in turn set up incentives and disincentives for political behavior (March and Olsen 1984). Particularly in societies deeply divided along ethnic or religious lines such as Bosnia (or other post-Ottoman countries, for example Lebanon or Iraq), there is interest in how the institutions can be designed, or engineered, to promote post-war statebuilding aims like more inclusive and consensual approaches to politics and policy. The purpose of institutional design is to engineer the political system to promote a common identity that reflects the reality of a common destiny. While traditional approaches have focused on the structure of the executive, the electoral system, and the territorial dispersion of power (through federalism or local decentralization), more recent research has focused on ways to regulate the political party system through clever design of party registration and other requirements (Reilly and Norlund 2008).

As a result, there has been a wide-ranging debate on the "best" institutions for countries emerging from war, especially those riven by identity-based conflict, and how they can serve statebuilding objectives by hard-wiring into the rules of the game incentives for inclusive politics. This work on engineering has prioritized especially the inclusion of all identity groups in society and mechanisms to protect the rights of minorities through features such as grand coalition governments, federalism and decentralization of power to local authorities, minority vetoes on issues of particular concern to them (and parallel structures for education or cultural matters, sometimes called "corporate federalism"), and through features such as collective presidencies or parliamentary systems that feature grand-coalition governments (Large and Sisk 2006). Some researchers also see power sharing in the military as a critical component of a broader power-sharing approach (Hartzell and Hodie 2007); these researchers and others overall report that a mix of power-sharing institutions does facilitate the consolidation of peace after civil war.[6]

The focus on power sharing is well and good because transitional moments present opportunities to redirect political systems in post-war countries so as to strengthen the ways they can serve as peaceful rules and processes to resolve underlying conflicts. In newly formed South Sudan, for example, there is an explicit recognition of the diversity and indeed diversification of power in the ten federal states. Federalism seems appropriate to the vast size of the new state, and to the realities of local authority that have deep historical roots and the identities of which are essential to understanding the identity dimensions that drove the country's decades of civil war (Deng 1995). Yet federalism (and power sharing in general) is no panacea, as the challenges of statebuilding at the national level are replicated, in a way, in the federal states as they seek to create regional institutions to govern effectively, and to develop subsequent levels of the state in terms of local governments.

Like South Sudan, many post-war countries wrestle with the question of federalism and decentralization of state power. In Nepal, federalism is advocated as a way to decentralize authority and give rights to long-disadvantaged caste and ethnic groups, although some are concerned it will lead to Maoist "capture" of local government structures and may indeed ignite new, localized conflicts. In Iraq, federalism became a lightning rod in the constitutional talks and eventually an "asymmetric" federal formula emerged that gives exceptional autonomy to the Kurdistan Regional Government. In DRC, given its history of secessionist civil war (the country saw civil war in 1960–4 during the Katanga crisis), the question of federalism has been equally problematic, as there is a constant tension between the need to strengthen a weak central state (that barely rules beyond the capital city of Kinshasa) and the need to devolve power to regional governments. In Bosnia, too, the federal formula (that provides for a Bosnia-Croat federation and a Republic Serbska) has been widely criticized as territorialization of ethnic separation that occurred during the war, yet now in place has created the conditions for its own perpetuation.

While adoption of federalism and autonomy are often necessary to end the war, it is not clear that the federal formula also contributes to the countervailing goal of statebuilding. The danger is that, as in Ethiopia, federalism can build unity in a multiethnic state – the victorious EPRDF adopted "ethnic federalism" after its civil war, including in the constitution the right to secession – or can reinforce ethnic divisions and fail to create a sense of common identity by emphasizing the "ethnicization" of public discourse (Fessha 2008: 519).

These debates on what types of institutions best contribute to peace have evolved to speak more in terms of *options* for post-war constitution-making processes rather than prescriptions.[7] Because of the local variance in key factors, such as the spatial distribution of identity groups or the historical experiences with various institutions – it is impossible to say there is a "one-size-fits-all" institutional design for post-war countries. Moreover, outsiders do not choose institutions in post-war contexts (with the exception of some cases like Bosnia of externally imposed peace); instead, the protagonists choose institutions, either through bargaining in the South Africa or Nepal examples, or through imposition by victors in the case of Ethiopia. Whether or not inclusive institutions emerge that are engineered for ameliorating conflict in post-war countries (and achieving other desiderata, such as facilitating development) depends on the preferences, power, and positions of local actors ... not on blueprints imported from abroad or the admonitions of foreign scholars and constitutional consultants.

Thus, international assistance to constitution-making bodies has moved to focus as a priority on the *process* of constitution making, and particularly ways to improve citizen participation in what is historically an elite-driven and secretive process (as was the 1987 Constitutional Convention in the United States, negotiated only by men and from which the media were barred). Today, participatory approaches to constitution making offer the opportunity for direct citizen input, extensive media coverage, and the direct participation of civil society in the deliberations. International support for constitution-making processes thus now adopts dual strategic approaches: technical assistance to key negotiators that present and evaluate institutional options in relation to a specific context, perhaps with some persuasion to adopt those institutions that outsiders may think are more appropriate; and support for a broader participatory process of local constitution making, so that new rules of the game can genuinely reflect a new social contract between the citizen and the state.[8]

Electoral Processes and Legislative Strengthening

The debate on democratization and statebuilding is nowhere more starkly presented than in the discourse around electoral processes at war's end. There are critiques that post-war elections are often foisted on fragile countries by outsiders in pursuit of an ideologically informed idea that elections will serve the purposes of creating the conditions for exit by international peacekeepers (or occupiers) or that elections put a country on the path to being a peaceful democracy over time. As in the section above, these debates relate to the sequencing of democratization and statebuilding and ultimately these goals are often seen as competing and mutually exclusive.

However, as in constitution making, there is often a myth that elections are transplanted from outside and the local parties bow to Western aid conditionality to undertake electoral processes. In reality, the terms of electoral processes are either set by victorious regimes when civil wars end in military victory (as in Rwanda, which held post-war, post-genocide elections for the president in 2003, won by incumbent Paul Kagame with 95.1 percent of the vote), or as a stipulation in peace agreements, for example the 2005 elections in Liberia which were agreed to in the Comprehensive Peace Agreement of 2003.[9] Thus, while the claim that external actors impose elections on post-war countries may be the case in some instances of transitional administration and occupation, the claim belies a much more varied reality, in which the international community often supports electoral processes which the parties themselves have the greatest motivation to conduct.

Four critical issues arise in considering electoral processes in post-conflict countries. The first, and arguably the most important, is the choice of an electoral system, which as Sartori has claimed is the "most specific, manipulable element of politics" (Sartori 1968: 273). The electoral system choice is important, even critical, because the electoral system is often a key determinant, over time, of the nature of the party system; and election systems can determine key issues such as the degree of inclusion and exclusion of political parties, the extent to which votes cast result in proportional or majoritarian distribution of seats in legislatures, and the effects of the electoral rules on issues such as women's participation. Generally, the literature has shown that highly majoritarian systems such as first-past-the-post are ill-suited to the needs of post-war countries, in part because these systems can lead to "permanent majorities" when voters vote along identity lines, or, similarly, "permanently excluded minorities." As a result, there is a propensity for international specialists, and sometimes international mediators, to recommend the use of party-list proportional representation in which there is closer fit to achieving a more even ratio of votes cast to seats won. While proportional representation may not yet be the default model for post-war countries, there are many who believe that it should be the choice for both post-war countries and other "new democracies" (Lijphart 2004).

Overall, election system choice is indeed critical, and there is good reason to lean toward proportional models that are inclusive. Yet as in institutional design more broadly, external actors do not always have much influence in electoral system choice. In the run-up to the 2005 elections in Afghanistan, key players such as the European Union, the United States, or the UN urged President Hamid Karzai to choose party-list PR. The thinking was that it is the most inclusive and that broader inclusion in the parliament (the Loya Jirga) might lessen the appeal of spoilers such as the Taliban. Yet Karzai opted for a complicated and somewhat rare system, the single non-transferable vote (SNTV), a candidate-based system which did not depend explicitly on the formation of political parties. Because the system features high district magnitude (number of candidates elected from each district), the choice for SNTV was fairly inclusive and did in fact yield a relatively high number of women winning seats. Scholar Astri Suhrke argues, though, that at the end of the day, Karzai's state-building logic was at deep odds with the outsiders' goal of democratizing Afghanistan. She observes that:

> Without electoral recognition of political parties, the parliament was likely to be fragmented and weak, with little capacity to aggregate local interests, address national-level issues, provide clear lines of accountability to the voters and thus, in the end, check the power of the executive branch. It would resemble the weak assembly during the democratic decade under Zahir Shah, and for some of the same reasons: the King had not allowed formal political parties at all for fear this would limit his own power. As an instrument to foster unity in a plural society, the SNTV was useless. For this purpose, a party-based proportional representation system would have been more suitable (Suhrke 2007: 10).

The Afghan example underscores that the key institutional choice of an electoral system depends often on expectations of the protagonists on how it may work for them over time, and not on a construct of what constitutes international best practice as such.

The second area in electoral processes is equally the question of election administration and the implications of what are often perceived as technical aspects of voting processes. For example, voter registration in post-war countries is especially problematic: often the legal framework is contentious, particularly on the question of citizenship; voter registration is highly political, and there may be efforts to prevent registration in certain areas by making them unsafe for election-support workers; and voter registration is often based on a prior census, which in many post-war countries has either not occurred recently, or at all. As well, when there are large communities of displaced persons, voter registration can be problematic if there are requirements for individuals to register or to vote in their home districts.[10]

The third critical area is institutionalizing the integrity of electoral processes over time, which requires the creation and indeed political protection of autonomous election-management bodies (typically independent election commissions). In countries such as Afghanistan, Cambodia, Liberia, or Sierra Leone, the first electoral process emerging from civil war is often mostly or wholly conducted by the United Nations. Beyond this first election, however, the creation of a vibrant democracy requires the ownership and conduct of the electoral process by national authorities. Election management bodies need capacity to conduct voter registration, to design ballots that are contextually appropriate, to register and regulate political parties, and to actually conduct the election. Critically important, as well, is their ability to adjudicate post-election disputes and investigate claims of fraud, intimidation, and vote rigging. The integrity and legitimacy of ruling regimes often rests directly on the credibility of this institution.

A final area for elections is the critical task of election-related security. In countries where the police have long served the interest of the ruling regime, or where new police forces are deployed following reintegration and security sector reform, challenges abound. The focus on election security involves upfront training and capacity building of the police regarding their role in securing the electoral process, measures for the capacity to secure and protect campaign rallies and candidates (which are often targets of election-related violence), and securing polling sites and ensuring that it is safe for citizens to vote. Because election-related violence often has the effect of suppressing voter turnout, and particularly participation by women or vulnerable minorities, a secure election is key to the goal of inclusivity in the electoral process. As a result, there have been considerable efforts by international organizations to develop conflict assessment instruments to anticipate the escalation of election-related violence and to devise appropriate measures for conflict prevention.[11]

In the meantime, regrettably, there are few alternatives to international action when post-war elections go awry and electoral processes re-ignite conflict. In the DRC in 2006, despite the presence of some 15,000 European Union troops and the deployment of UN MONUSCO peacekeepers, election violence undermined the polls' credibility. There was escalating violence in the run-up to the election, during the first and second round of presidential voting, and after the polls, post election conflict erupted between backers of the putative winner, President Joseph Kabila, and his opponent, Jean-Marie Bemba. Bemba had won most of eastern DRC, while Kabila carried the west. Overall, the violence marred the credibility of the poll, called into question the considerable investment of cash and human capacity in the event, and in retrospect – as violence again marred the 2011 poll, which was widely seen as fraudulently ill-administered – raises questions about the entire exercise of holding elections in conditions such as obtain in the DRC.

On the other hand, it is also clear that electoral processes can be real turning points in the direction of recovery of the authority of the state and a renegotiation of the social contract. In South Africa, the electoral moment of 1994 was in fact the tipping point through which the state was restructured after decades of internal strife, and which in turn has offered an opportunity for strengthening the state in its relations with society (du Toit 1995). In Liberia, elections in 2005 that brought the first female president of an African country, Ellen Johnson Sirleaf (re-elected in 2011), gave the country a real start at statebuilding for the first time in modern history. Similarly, the credibility of the electoral management body in neighboring Sierra Leone is also credited with giving that country a chance to find political stability, even when incumbent regimes lose; in 2007, the country managed a political transition through which the former opposition party, now-President Earnest Bai Koromo's All People's Congress, replaced the former ruling regime (former President Ahmad Tejan Kabbah's Sierra Leone People's Party, which won UN-conducted elections in 2002).

Similarly, in Libya in 2012, an independent electoral commission managed to administer post-war elections in a remarkably capable fashion (with considerable technical assistance from outside), even though some militias in eastern parts of the country threatened to disrupt the polls. A peaceful election and a legitimating of interim rule in Libya bode well as a start to what will be a monumental statebuilding task, beginning with security sector reform.

Elections are the gateway to power, and because those with power in post-war countries have often been tied to armed militias, militaries, or rebel factions, there is broad concern that representative democracy in such contexts can lead to "warlord democracy" (Wantchekon 2004). Candidates and power brokers with their armed militias and private security forces may mean that post-war parliaments are not necessarily representative of social interests as a whole, and indeed the allocation of power along such lines has been seen as inhibitive of statebuilding in post-war countries such as Afghanistan, Lebanon, Liberia, and Iraq. The anemic, divided, weak, and sometimes powerless roles of post-war legislatures in the face of a real political game outside of parliament means that efforts to build a democratic state often run aground in the poor capacity of legislatures to function as means of oversight. Thus, the notion of a formal "horizontal" accountability by parliamentary institutions of executives or of ministries essentially run by a faction or identity group (for example, in power-sharing contexts like Lebanon) is weak if not absent in many post-war countries.

Legislative strengthening is thus inherently a difficult and long-term task, and support for legislative institutions by outside donors is fraught with strategic and operational conundrums. Most assistance goes to areas such as remediating legal and administrative staff and research-oriented capacities, together with capacity development for individual legislators and senior legislative directors. However, the difficult part is very much strengthening the capacity of the legislature to function in critical areas of fiscal policy management (i.e., drafting and passing a budget), in investigation and oversight functions, and – most importantly – in overcoming internal divisions, factionalism, and identity-based politics.[12] Moreover, parliaments should play a role in key areas such as security sector reform, formulation of national development strategies, and social policy to reintegrate war veterans. Critical to progress in the very difficult area of legislative strengthening is the work of the global Inter-Parliamentary Union, which has been involved in legislative strengthening in post-war countries and has emerged as a leader in the community of practice aimed at improving parliamentary capacities after civil war.

Because of the distrust in formal institutions, in Guatemala a process of democratic dialogue has been instrumental in addressing the complex relations that resonate across economic, social, and political contexts; the process involved former guerillas, representatives of the state, civil society, academics, and local and traditional leaders. The Guatemala dialogue produced pathways to social cohesion and to inclusive statebuilding in reports such as the "*Visión Guatemala 1998–2000*" that presented a roadmap to rebuilding state–society relations after conflict, and to building an inclusive state to overcome historical divisions along identity lines.[13] The Guatemala example points the way toward an evolving approach to statebuilding that is reconciled with the core international principles of, and local aspirations for, democracy.

Rule of Law, Human Rights, and Access to Justice

Democracy is meaningless without a basic floor of human rights and the rule of law. Moreover, states today have myriad international legal obligations to promote and uphold universal human rights, to include the rights of women (including prevention of gender-based violence and punishment of perpetrators), protection of religious minorities and freedom of discrimination on the basis of belief, and the rights of vulnerable persons such as those who are HIV-positive. Rule of law institutions are central to all aspects of statebuilding, including accountability as to the use of the state's authority, combating crime that undermines development, and the creation or strengthening of institutions through which there are opportunities to resolve social conflict non-violently. For this reason, rule of law components are common elements of statebuilding projects, and they have featured prominently in external efforts to build states in countries such as Afghanistan, Burundi, DRC, Haiti, Liberia, and South Sudan.[14]

Several findings resonate in the experience to promote rule of law. The first is that countries emerging from conflict inevitably face difficult decisions on transitional justice, both in terms of the extent and nature of prosecution of war-time atrocities but also the often selective and incomplete nature of such prosecutions. The rich literature on transitional justice would suggest that the aim of "ending impunity" is a laudable one, and that even the ritual of a process through which the perpetrators of gross violations of human rights are brought to account is a critical precursor to democratization; without at least some minimal notion of reconciliation, there can be no trust in democratic processes. However, actually measuring empirically the impact of transitional justice on the long-term sustainability of peace has been difficult to conduct empirically (Van der Merwe et al. 2009).

The second is that many practitioners, at least, recognize that the now-common model of a Truth and Reconciliation Commission, the mechanism used in democratizing Chile or post-war/democratizing South Africa, is not a one-size-fits-all solution that can be dropped into other social contexts. For example, the transitional justice commission in Liberia has been a deeply troubled institution, and its report was widely seen as being more problematic to peace than contributing to national reconciliation, particularly in its efforts to ban popular politicians from public life (including President Sirleaf).[15] When pursuing transitional justice, it is now important to consider that there are a variety of models, along national lines, hybrid international-national models (such as the International Commission against Impunity in Guatemala, or CICIG), and mostly international prosecution through the ICC.[16]

As in other areas, rule-of-law institutions such as the

courts, legal institutions such as bar societies, or implementing institutions such as the police (see chapter 3) are weak,
compromised, and underresourced. Furthermore, before and
during conflict, it is likely that informal service providers from
traditional authorities, religious authorities, or non-statutory
community courts have dispensed justice and adjudicated
disputes (International Institute for Democracy and Election
Assistance (IDEA) 2009). It is therefore difficult at best to talk
about human rights in such contexts when there is little institutionalization of the formal justice sector and many people
turn to informal institutions. Thus, in evaluating the extent
to which rule of law can be improved, and human rights
protected, in countries emerging from conflict is to improve
citizen access to justice, to begin a new human rights culture,
and to address directly the cultural and informal institutions
that are barriers to progress on human rights (for example,
religious courts that do not recognize sufficiently the rights of
women).

A third finding is that rule of law is very much about access
to justice. This is true for everyone, but especially for women.
Women's rights and attention to women's issues such as
the prevention and punishment of gender-based violence,
women's ability to access justice providers, and the design
and adjudication of family law and property rights are the
critical linchpins for advancement of women's development
more broadly. UNDP's Practice Note on Access to Justice
acknowledges that:

> There is a general tendency for access to justice reform (both
> multilateral and bilateral) to focus on programs supporting
> formal mechanisms of justice, especially processes of adju-
> dication through the judiciary. This is understandable from
> a governance perspective. However, from access to justice
> perspectives, it is essential that common parameters of
> assessment be applied to both formal and informal justice

mechanisms. Hence, UNDP's approach to justice sector reform focuses on strengthening the independence and integrity of both formal and informal justice systems, making both more responsive and more effective in meeting the needs of justice for all – especially the poor and marginalized (United Nations Development Program 2004: 4).

In balancing between formal and informal justice institutions, one of the most difficult tasks is to identify those informal processes that may be more consistent with international human rights, and those that by virtue of culture or conviction are less amenable to global norms and state obligations. Operationally, this often means balancing human rights, peacebuilding, and statebuilding objectives, such that human rights promoters have recognized that hybrid formal and informal domestic courts are likely to persist and that progress in access to justice may require working more initially with informal actors at the outset (and accepting their disconnect with global norms) and working to empower the formal judicial sector over time. In this regard, one of the most promising avenues is the early creation of new institutions in post-war societies to advance a culture of human rights and to monitor compliance with human rights norms. Human rights commissions have proven useful in the most difficult contexts: the Afghanistan Independent Human Rights Commission, for example, has issued regular monitoring reports and has begun the process of reporting compliance with international human rights treaties.[17]

Finally, it is impossible to achieve security, development, or democracy in conditions rife with corruption. Anti-corruption efforts in fragile countries has been one of the most difficult areas of the statebuilding enterprise, in part because corruption as a practice is both a form of informal institution (a set of rules of the game) and often a function of a culture of impunity for graft, influence, and patronage peddling, and distribution of public resources along narrow identity-based lines. Typically, outsiders seek to build a public administration that is well paid (in order to reduce the temptation of corruption), to promote participatory budgeting, transparency in procurement, and ways to audit and oversee revenue and spending and especially the management of natural-resource export-fed sovereign wealth funds. In finding innovative ways to support local or internal capacities to fight corruption, increasingly outsiders look for those nodes or "islands" of integrity within existing judicial systems, within civil society organizations or the media, as a way to build on what exists within society as an approach to improving performance in anti-corruption efforts.[18]

In Iraq, for example, it was seen that the Board of Supreme Audit, located within the judiciary, had managed to retain some degree of public trust and integrity through the years of the Saddam Hussein dictatorship. Although Iraqi law covers most requirements of the United Nations Convention against Corruption, which has been signed and ratified by Iraq, backing agencies that are designed to prevent corruption with financial support – such as the Board of Supreme Audit – has seen only modest results.[19] Iraq did develop a new National Anti-Corruption Strategy and Action Plan in 2009, but the lack of a strong social contract between the people and the state – a "tax-mediated social contract" – weakens the watchdog role of official anti-corruption organizations and agencies, civil society, and the media. As David Lake argues, the US intervention in Iraq to build a state after Saddam Hussein's fall was fraught with folly; he argues that US statebuilding efforts amounted to an "utter failure;" his research underscored the inherent tensions in the statebuilding-by-outsiders perspective, and he argues that statebuilding is unlikely to succeed when intervention is driven more by the putative global interests of a great power to create a regional client state than by an endogenous or internally led statebuilding process (Lake 2013).

Civil Society and Social Cohesion

States cannot be effective without strong societies. Without local ownership and local-level processes of security, reconciliation, and development, peacebuilding is not sustainable. In the context of weak state capacities, moreover, developing more enduring state–society relations requires an on-the-ground strategy of civil society building that cross-cuts lines of conflict and promotes more conflict-mitigating intergroup relations by building an integrated civil society, not sectarian organizations (Paris 2004: 194–6). Thus, the statebuilding perspective involves not just the revival and reconfiguration of the authoritative institutions and processes of governance, but the much broader, longer-term, and development-oriented goals of social transformation in creating autonomous, independent organizations of civil society that can engage the government and hold it to account, and indeed at the same time participate in the policy-making process and oversee the state's implementation of it.

Approaches to relying on informal institutions such as traditional authorities to provide access to justice, as described above, reflect a much broader problem. Direct support to civil society can legitimize and strengthen informal structures in society at the expense of the state, which ultimately has legal and practical responsibility for service delivery and in authoritatively adjudicating the law (Unsworth 2010). Thus, outsiders often face a dilemma between supporting the state directly to bolster its capacity, or investing more in local civil society and community-based approaches as an alternative, or counter-balance, to state power. Support to civil society through aid flows in post-war countries departs from a perspective of their being the principal institutions on the ground with the capability of delivering services. Many donors and international NGOs prefer to work directly with society-based organizations, bypassing the often corrupt institutions of the state, particularly at the local level where government capacity is often weakest.

In addition to the dilemma of empowering society at the expense of the state, donors also face a number of challenges in working with and indeed directly supporting civil society organizations. The first is one of analysis, in that the international community often lacks a good understanding of the nature of civil society, and the extent to which any particular organization can make a valid claim toward local access, legitimacy, and authenticity. This means that in working with civil society, it is really a donor-by-donor, case-by-case analysis of the capacity of these organizations to actually deliver services in areas that international organizations or the state cannot reach. In the critical area of health care, for example, USAID has often found that the best means of delivering needed aid supplies and medicines for health-care delivery has been through civil society, while recognizing that this direct support is ultimately vexatious; in a cross-national comparison of civil society and health-care delivery in Afghanistan, Cambodia, Mozambique, and Timor-Leste, USAID found that such donor support for civil society to deliver services may ultimately undermine the social contract:

> Donors may fuel the growth of the non-state sector, but governments also play a role. The governments studied here have their own set of suspicions about homegrown NGOs (which have proliferated over time in response to market forces) and have sought in different ways to delimit the space for NGOs as civil society agents. In the past, tensions between NGOs and government tended to focus on voice, rights, and participation in the political process . . .

Today the tension may be more about control over resources and the political leverage this imputes. Insofar as service delivery efficiencies are a legitimating force, it is no wonder that governments feel this way. As state-avoidance strategies drive resource flows into the non-state sector, weak or weakening public sector capacity becomes part of an unhelpful self-fulfilling rationalization on the part of donors for continued state circumvention. It also underscores state suspicions about civil society (USAID and the BASICS Project 2006: 30).

From an explicitly democracy-building point of view, civil society is expected to play two critical roles: first, in terms of providing vertical accountability, or the accountability of the state to its people, and in terms of providing for the cross-cutting of identity divisions or other conflict cleavages in society. Indeed, research from India has shown that inter-communal violence is less likely in those situations where civil society cross-cuts identity lines (in this case, along Hindu–Muslim lines) (Varshney 2001).

Civil society's role in providing accountability is also problematic. While local civil society organizations have done amazing work in documenting human rights abuses by the state, in calling the state to account through local research on service delivery failures or problems such as corruption, and in aspects of social accountability such as participatory election monitoring, there are reasons to be sanguine about the extent to which organizations can actually perform these tasks in conflict-affected regions.

One reason for caution is that civil society itself may be divided along conflict lines, and there is very little cross-cutting civil society to be found. Indeed, a characteristic of post-war countries is often parallel civil society organizations that may or may not be conducive to peace, in the case of Bosnia for example (Belloni 2008). Belloni also reviews experiences from cases in Africa, and from Sri Lanka and Northern Ireland in which civil society organizations have served primarily to strengthen their bonding ties along identity and kinship lines – which in turn exacerbated conflict dynamics – instead of service to cross-stitch across lines of conflict in society.

Thania Paffenholz and Christoph Spurk found in their study for the World Bank that while civil society does have an important role to play in peacebuilding, it can have a "dark side." They report that

> There is some evidence that effective service delivery adds to the legitimacy of civil society actors, but there is also evidence that service delivery does not necessarily enhance civic engagement. In addition, some cases show that fostering representative civil society need not be accompanied by service delivery. There are also concerns that advocacy work is deemphasized when civil society organizations are driven into service delivery and thus drawn away from other important functions, or that service delivery is weakened or at least discredited when it is not linked to advocacy (Paffenholz and Spurk 2006: 36–7).

Statebuilding objectives may require a shift toward supporting those civil society organizations that are explicitly cross-cutting of identity lines, and that can serve to represent interests in society that transcend lines of conflict. This is not an easy task, but in some more historical cases such as South Africa, this donor strategy of rewarding and indeed incentivizing cross-cutting civil society was the key to successful democratization over time.[20] As well, the practice of infusing conflict management and negotiation training to create such bridging institutions in civil society has come a long way: Martina Fischer of the Berlin-based Berghof Center on Conflict Transformation has found that, ultimately, civil society participation in building state capacities in countries emerging from civil war is critical. In her extensive study, focusing especially on the case of Bosnia and the broader experience in the Balkans, Fischer concludes that:

> Civil society cannot be "created" entirely from the outside. External support can only strengthen local capacities: if no such capacities exist, nothing can be strengthened. Further, international interventions should provide incentives for cooperation between state and non-state actors. In order to create effective partnerships for peace, and effective networks of action, transnational NGOs must comply with certain "codes of conduct" so as to avoid the destructive dynamics of "insider-outsider" relationships. International and transnational NGOs have to make sure that they do not undermine the efforts of local civil society peace initiatives which are working in the conflict situation, especially by imposing their own agendas (2006: 24).

Conclusion

Democracy in post-war contexts is not uniformly imposed from abroad, as is wrongly assumed. Many Afghan women, for example, have gained rights through a democratization agenda, and they worry that negotiations with the Taliban to reverse this progress may lead to a restriction of these rights.[21] The pressures by outsiders and insiders alike for a quick turn to democratic processes is reflective of the critical role that democratic processes and respect for human rights plays in imbuing the post-war state with some semblance of legitimacy and in addressing the needs of the vulnerable or oppressed segments of populations. In the twenty-first century, the idea that countries emerging from war can defer democracy in general, and elections specifically, until the state is built, is a fallacious proposition. States, and the governmental elites who rule them, crave the legitimacy that only elections can seemingly provide. While cautious, international support for statebuilding, then, has to be about confirming and reinforcing global democratic norms and the internal demands for democratic rights from the most vulnerable in society, even in the most inhospitable environments for them.

That does not mean, however, that there should be uncritical support for electoral processes based on unrealistic expectations or impossible timetables ... especially when such timetables are generated by exit-strategy designs from outside. Indeed, what is needed is greater ability to assess when electoral processes will induce conflict, and when they will sharpen divisions and lead to violence. The crisis that developed in the Côte d'Ivoire in 2010 is indicative of the kind of violent imbroglios that can emerge when the institutions of the state are weak and where elections are perceived as a fight-to-the-death effort to control the commanding heights of power. At the end of the day, the crisis was finally resolved by the UN's enforcement, together with a colonial-era power (in this case, France), military force proving the way to enforce the outcomes of a UN-verified election conducted under the eye of a UN peacekeeping force (UNOCI). Some 3,000 lives were lost in the violent confrontation to enforce the outcome of the election, and the International Criminal Court's Chief Prosecutor, Luis Moreno-Ocampo, has alleged that both sides committed war crimes during the brief but intense conflict.[22]

The Côte d'Ivoire experience also reinforces that building democratic states after civil war requires much more emphasis on consensual democracy and electoral processes that are more about representation than they are unfettered access to the pinnacles of state power through majority rule (and especially presidential) elections. Elections should be developed in a way to be as inclusive as possible, which suggests in most circumstances some form of proportional representation system combined with parliamentary executives. But inclusivity can also lead to paralysis. It took Iraq nine months to form a government following the elections of March 2010, and during that time the uncertainty contributed to the chronic insecurity and violence that has accompanied transition and statebuilding in Iraq.[23]

Thus, there are trade-offs to be considered in each case by policymakers trying to balance inclusivity aims with government effectiveness criteria. Among the most important risks to inclusivity are the inability to forge political coalitions that can create national vision and a sense of common destiny; often, power-sharing institutions that emerge from war are more about power dividing, and instead of building an authoritative state it becomes rather permanently disabled as an autonomous, neutral institution. Inclusion is critical for legitimacy of the state, and so assessing electoral processes must start from this value, rather than the other values that elections are supposed to perform (such as providing accountability or local-area voice through locally chosen representatives). Legislatures are likely to be weak, divided, and challenged with performing basic tasks. Civil society is equally no panacea, and often it, too, is unable to perform as a check against state power. Thus, building state capacities and desiderata like inclusivity may work at cross-purposes.

Perhaps the best approach to reconciling the statebuilding and democracy-building approach is to emphasize the concept and process of democracy as a dialogue.[24] Overcoming conflict requires more than just one-off attempts at "reconciliation," but an ongoing proliferation of opportunities to bargain among conflicting social forces, to provide a place at the decision-making table for minorities, women, or other historically disadvantaged groups, and to approach statebuilding as a more relational approach at the society level. The democratic dialogue approach has proven to be an important instrument for placing electoral processes and human rights into a broader social project, and the international role has been important in this approach.

CHAPTER SEVEN

Strengthening the International Statebuilding Regime

While new states may still form occasionally and eventually be recognized in the international system, as South Sudan was in 2011, the process of state formation globally seems mostly complete. Whatever new states may emerge in the coming years, they are likely to be few, and they are likely to happen in those areas where there are already existing separatist tendencies or unresolved sovereignty claims (as in Western Sahara or perhaps South Ossetia in Georgia), or perhaps through "velvet divorces" like the unlikely independence of Scotland in a popular referendum.[1]

Thus, a critical peace and security task of the twenty-first century is to build the authority, capacity, and legitimacy of those states that presently enjoy formal, legal recognition as sovereign entities but which in reality are deeply fragile in the wake of war. Weak state authority, legitimacy, and capacity in fragile and conflict-affected countries are a principal barrier to realizing a twenty-first century which sees an end of chronic poverty and the horrors of civil war. Indeed, today's principal man-made humanitarian emergencies – such as the nearly 21 million refugees and displaced persons at risk in 2012 – are the consequences of conflict in these failed-state countries.

But states that garner their authority solely from formal-legal international recognition, that survive by means of aid flows and security protection from foreign powers, and that fail to deliver basic public services to their citizens, are castles made of sand. Without internal, domestic authority that comes from citizen consent of the state's right to rule, without the ability of the state to create an enabling environment for economic vitality and livelihoods for the poorest and most vulnerable segments of the population, and without legitimacy that flows from a truly democratic social contract, states are vulnerable to violent challenges to their rule through armed insurgency or to capture by predatory, criminal elites.

Consequently, the future of the twenty-first century depends highly on the success of statebuilding in the conflict-affected, least-developing countries, the "fragile states." Processes such as the MDGs and the post-MDG framework in 2015 will drive a focus on governance and the state as it becomes increasingly clear that countries falling behind on the goals to cut chronic poverty are conflict-ridden. Global dialogue and donor–recipient state dialogue processes such as the International Dialogue on Peacebuilding and Statebuilding offer new avenues and mechanisms for developing more effective aid and resolving some of the dilemmas of local ownership.

Reinvigorating the Responsibility to Protect

As highlighted in the Introduction, the post-Cold War era of threats to international peace and security emanating from civil wars and internal conflicts has in turn precipitated the creation of a global regime to address, first, peacebuilding in the wake of war, and, over the longer term, statebuilding to consolidate the peace. Like other "global governance" regimes, this means setting an agenda at the highest levels of international policy to create consensus on the role of the international community to respond in cases where the state fails to govern, or when it turns its monopoly of violence against its own people. Global governance regimes are also about the creation and codification of international rules or norms, both "hard" (formal-legal) and "soft" international law (guidelines), which, in application to domestic contexts, are about articulating internationalized standards about what constitutes responsible exercise of sovereignty and the obligations of states to comply with international charters on human rights. International regimes also entail monitoring for compliance by the international community and local actors in new ways that involve citizen participation and social accountability (see chapter 6). Finally, a global regime for improving governance and facilitating statebuilding involves aid and support to help build compliance by states with international norms and to react to non-compliance in those cases where states fail utterly to act consistent with international norms.

In terms of agenda setting, nothing underscores more the changing nature of international scrutiny than when the state fails in its responsibilities. First among the evolution of norms in recent years has been the evolving doctrine of the "responsibility to protect" (R2P), which asserts that states committing gross atrocities against their own citizens cannot hide behind the shield of sovereignty. In the case of Libya in 2011, for example, a brutal dictatorship, wallowing in oil wealth and enforcing its rule through clan-based local legitimacy and paid mercenaries from abroad, began to commit gross violations of human rights as the Arab Spring uprisings spread from Tunisia, to Egypt, and to Libya. As the Libyan armed forces began to kill civilians in Benghazi following Qadhafi's pledge on February 15, 2011, to "cleanse Libya house by house" until protestors surrendered, and the armed forces began using human shields to protect themselves from the incipient insurgency to oust the regime, R2P was invoked as the basis for a collective global response to the Libya crisis.

The international community began to react first through regional organizations such as the Arab League and the African Union, and eventually at the pinnacle of global power in the UN Security Council. UN Security Council Resolution 1973, adopted March 18, 2011, asserted that the Libyan state may have committed crimes against humanity and authorized international intervention under Chapter VII of the charter and in particular to protect civilians. The NATO campaign that ensued was pivotal in creating the conditions through which Libyan society could rise up and overthrow the dictatorship and begin the process of creating a new government and indeed negotiating a new social contract.

The Libyan case – followed on quickly by the crisis in Syria – underscores the need for continued evolution of the global statebuilding regime, particularly in the ability to respond when states turn their capacity to kill on their own people. At the level of agenda setting, it is quite clear that the norm of state sovereignty continues to change rapidly. Although more powerful states such as China or Russia may be less pervious to global intervention, the rules of the global game are clearly changing, and gross violations of human rights by states are no longer tolerable in terms of the evolving doctrine of R2P. At the same time, the realities of geopolitics in Syria in 2012 – where UNSC permanent members Russia and China blocked a robust intervention – suggest that there is still a long way to go before the R2P norm is consistently put into practice and the UN or its member states have the capacity and willingness to regularly apply it.

This evolving norm, however, raises hopes about the future of international intervention to arrest state failure and to protect civilians when the state is culpable in gross violations of human rights. While the political will to intervene in Libya was present, in other cases – such as in Syria, or earlier in Iran in light of its repression following the 2010 election, or in Zimbabwe where a repressive regime has killed and detained thousands in the late 2000s – there is no automaticity to international responses. Typically, where there is little political will for international military intervention, the international community tends to rely on targeted sanctions against ruling elites and on weaker measures such as "naming and shaming." While these half-step measures do help further undermine the legitimacy of the regime that has captured the state, they are inherently limited in their effects, and authoritarian or predatory governments often find ways to evade or buffer the effects of sanctions.

It may well be that in the long run, evolving doctrines like R2P may have a deterrent effect against repression and may indirectly aid in the building of a truly consistent global regime to prevent states from oppressing their own societies. Some attribute the rapid and remarkable reforms launched by the government of Myanmar in late 2011, which has embarked on negotiations with the opposition parties (led by Nobel Peace Laureate Aung San Suu Kyi), as a possible indication of the effect of R2P as an evolving norm in affecting the internal dynamics of statebuilding in cases of fragility.

Thus, global norms like R2P continue to evolve beyond the early evocation of the initial principles of humanitarian intervention, reflecting an enduring concern of outsiders to intervene in costly civil wars to stem mass atrocities (Weiss 2004). The rub, however, comes when considering the actual *modus vivendi* of international intervention. What is clear is that military intervention by foreign forces, whether they are international peacekeepers in the case of Timor-Leste, or an international coalition led by a powerful state in the case of Afghanistan (see chapter 4), military intervention is at best an emergency response to prevent the worst implications of state failure or the spillover of conflict onto the global stage. Although today military interventions are "complex" and they include significant, early support to reinstate the rule of law, to demobilize and reintegrate former fighters, to build the administrative edifice of the state, and to launch democracy (often through internationally administered elections), military intervention alone cannot build states. One of the most important goals of peacekeeping today is to consider how civilian components of such complex missions can better set the stage for rapid recovery of the state's autonomy and the extension of state authority, capacity, and legitimacy over time.[2]

At best, military intervention can resolve local security dilemmas and allow for a period of initial recovery to stabilize and reconstruct the state. But outsiders cannot build states on their own, or even be in the driver's seat. As the examples of Afghanistan and Iraq have shown, where the US has foundered in achieving the more political aims of its intervention in these countries, statebuilding cannot be imposed from abroad by force alone: unless states are built on the basis of a domestic social contract, they are castles made of sand that may well dissolve rapidly in renewed conflict once the external interveners depart.

Improving External Aid Effectiveness in Post-war Countries

International development aid to states must be made more effective and efficient; large-scale efforts involving military intervention and "nation-building" aid, in particular, have proven to be a drastic failure in terms of aid effectiveness and program and project success. At the same time, practitioners point to effective historical interventions, such as in Mozambique or El Salvador, that demonstrate that over time international assistance is essential to creating strong institutions locally that – while imperfect – do provide for basic security and create the conditions for development. Thus, there is the need for stock-taking and new approaches in the field of statebuilding, and for new efforts to think and act more regionally in places where conflict spills across domestic boundaries – as in the "Horn of Africa," South Asia, or West Africa, and where regional solutions are required.

Aid is often ineffective because such resources create a political economy of dependency that can rearrange the accountability of state elites to donors rather to their own people. As well, aid has often been used to pursue quick fixes through capacity substitution – such as the deployment of international technical advisors in ministries or at the local level – rather than for capacity building. The inherent limits of outsiders to build states internally raise new questions about the efficacy of complementary international instruments to aid and accelerate a peaceful process of internal statebuilding. Improving international assistance requires further improvement in two areas: the efficacy of development assistance (aid) as a means of building state capacities, and improving approaches to local ownership and to local capacity building.

Today, the United Nations as a system, and indeed the entire array of global "development partners" – multilateral and bilateral aid agencies, is especially seized with the goals of improving aid efficacy and in new approaches to capacity building. Because bad governance is often at the heart of the problem of fragility in these countries, it is central to the UN's approach to building the local capacities of the state to manage conflict and to ameliorate underlying root causes of conflict.[3] The sheer quantity of aid flows seems to be insufficient to explain the extent of progress in statebuilding. Indeed, over the period 2003–11, Afghanistan and Iraq, respectively, have been at the top of the list of recipient states for international development aid (see chapter 1).

Moreover, there are differences within the aid community over what the baseline goals of statebuilding should be. Some, such as the World Bank, see "good governance" as a realistic aim, whereas the more normatively oriented actors such as the UNDP argue in favor of "democratic governance."[4]

There have been those who have argued for an even more minimalist goal in fragile states, such as "good enough governance," or, on the other hand, some bilateral donors such as the United States that come with a much more exhaustive goal of "democracy building." The lack of consensus among outsiders on the ultimate aims of development assistance to support the statebuilding objective is grounded in an acute appreciation of the scope of the enterprise, the long-term nature of the task, and the inability of outsiders to understand local dynamics and individual-level incentives of local elites to actually build the capacities of states. The incoherence of international responses is furthered by the fact that many new donors have entered the arena and now provide support directly or indirectly to fragile-state governments.

Among these important new development actors is China, which often has very little conditionality for its foreign direct investment and aid activities on issues of good governance or human rights, in turn often providing critical resources to fledgling governments without the strings attached by traditional Western OECD-DAC donors.[5] So, too, countries such as India and Brazil have also become important new donors. India, for example, created in 2012 a new Development Partnership Administration (DPA), which shifts its identity from aid recipient to aid provider and which illustrates well the new emphasis on "South-South" capacity building in which developing countries can learn better from each other (rather than from the West) on the statebuilding challenges for peace and development. As W. Pal Sidhu notes:

> India could learn from its own domestic nation building experience which, clearly, recognizes the important link between development and security. Although the Indian experience would be more relevant to other developing countries, harnessing it for the international arena is a challenge. It would depend on how well the DPA is able to

incorporate the relevant domestic talent for its international responsibilities.[6]

There is recognition in the aid community that conventional approaches to capacity building in fragile states are not working and that aid must become more effective. In a series of conclaves organized by the OECD-DAC, dialogues among donors and recipient states have begun to create a new agenda for aid. In 2005, donors adopted the Paris Declaration on Aid Effectiveness, which paired donor pledges for more aid with partner or beneficiary country pledges to improve governance and especially development performance. Paris began a process of mutual accountability between the donors and recipient governments as a way of creating new pathways of "local ownership" of the statebuilding process. The Paris Declaration was followed by a series of high-level forums of dialogue between the donors and recipients (together with representatives of global and local civil societies) with landmark declarations such as the Accra Agenda for Action in 2008, the Dili Declaration of 2010, the Monrovia Road Map of June 2011, and the "New Deal" declaration on common peacebuilding and statebuilding goals that emerged from the 2011 Busan High-Level Forum.[7]

These global dialogue processes on aid effectiveness provide an understanding of the direction of the statebuilding regime based on a dialogue between the outsider interveners and the local beneficiary states. Perhaps most promising in this dialogue is the active participation of the so-called G7+ group of representative "fragile" states (in late 2012, there were 17 members) in the dialogue. The "Monrovia Objectives" suggest a consensus of sorts on the goals of the statebuilding enterprise, consistent with the view of statebuilding presented in this book. They start with legitimacy and the importance of "inclusive political settlements," security through "people security," access to justice and not just the rule of law, employment and livelihoods as the basis for economic security, and ameliorating aid dependency and curbing corruption.[8]

Building on these lofty goals, which are increasingly shared by both the global and local actors in the statebuilding regime, suggests that future gains will be made not just at the level of normative developments, but most critically in new approaches to using aid effectively to build local capacities. Indeed, it is through building local capacities that the oft-vexatious principle of "local ownership" can be realized. Development of local capacities reflects the aim of enabling the state to fulfill its functions autonomously and without significant, direct international support and with the direct engagement of, and accountability to, its citizens. Thus, it is through capacity building that local actors and citizens can meaningfully exercise the shaping of national development agendas, specific policies and programs, and determine priorities. As highlighted in a UN DESA policy report, "The strengthening of state institutions requires political choices shaped by local values and conditions rather than general technocratic solutions."[9]

There remains a lack of systematic research and integrated understanding on how state and non-state capacity is affected by fragility and conflict, its influence on post-conflict recovery, and how capacity building can contribute most effectively to institutionalizing peace.[10] There is also the challenge of linking capacity development (conceptually and practically) to concepts such as statebuilding, which guide thinking and interventions by institutional actors in this area. Among the concerns are the degree of difficulty and complexity in state capacity building (through needs assessments or through capacity assessment frameworks, for example); the magnitude and nature of transformational change in state capacities (through evaluation of post-war transitional pathways, for example); and the timeframe for such transitions.[11]

While capacity building is often associated with the practicalities of the enterprise, and especially the role of advisors and trainers or in providing experts for specific technical assistance tasks, the concept and practice of capacity development is much broader. Fragile countries require a more careful understanding of what capacity development means and how it applies in the aftermath of conflict. As a World Bank report finds:

> It is often tempting for donors to try and bypass weak government capacity and attempt to rebuild the country themselves. In other words, to contract services directly and to provide assistance in kind. This is superficially attractive when government institutions are weak, skilled nationals are in shortly supply and the fiduciary systems that ensure that money goes to intended purposes are also weak . . . But country ownership matters in a post-war setting just as much, if not more, than under normal conditions for development. We have seen that when donors bypass national systems anticipated results do not take place.[12]

Accepting Hybridity and Ambiguous Outcomes

Building states and overcoming syndromes of fragility take time. No pre-set sequence or carefully laid plans and set of well-derived benchmarks can overcome the deep drivers of conflict, the social maladies of chronic poverty and exclusion, or the tendency of some state elites to become predatory over time. Thus, for the immediate term, it must be acknowledged that international efforts to build states through military intervention and occupation, through aid flows, and through capacity building will be incomplete and subject to reversals when the waves of social problems overwhelm the shaky structures of internationally supported state institutions.

In the immediate term, in fragile state contexts, outcomes of international intervention will be mixed at best and often of a "hybrid" nature, meaning that weak state institutions will exist side by side with informal institutions such as traditional leaders and religious authorities, criminal organizations, social self-help networks, and in some cases insurgent groups who hold territory and wield their own authority in proto-states (as in the FARC-controlled regions of Colombia). The hybridity argument seeks to capture the incomplete and often compromised outcomes that emerge in countries where the international community is engaged in helping to build peace but where local resistance to change frustrates progress toward statebuilding and democracy (MacGinty 2010). This suggests that at times the statebuilding imperative may overwhelm or trump the more norm-driven agendas of democracy building.

To overcome these capacity-building dilemmas, statebuilding in practice needs to be much more oriented to building on what exists rather than transplanting foreign models and processes into ill-suited local environments. This means first of all identifying better methods for understanding the appropriateness and abilities of local institutions that enjoy a modicum of legitimacy or that can efficiently deliver services. As a start, post-war needs assessment needs to reach out through structured dialogue processes to civil society (for example, traditional leaders, religious leaders), critical groups whose commitment to peace is essential and who may have the capacity to "spoil" (mid-level and rank-and-file ex-combatants), and especially vulnerable populations, such as refugees and other displaced persons, women, and youth.[13]

Rightly, outsiders focus on leaders and indeed on building leadership capacities. The focus on individual capacities in post-war settings is guided by the premise that, first, leadership is a critical variable in the advancement of peace after conflict; time and again, leadership qualities of responsibility, consensus building, inclusion, vision, and integrity have proven critical in post-war settings.[14] Recent approaches to strategic engagement at the leadership level in post-war societies address directly the relational dimensions of leadership, for example across ethnic, regional, religious, or other conflict divisions, as the essential ingredient of an effective peacebuilding approach.[15]

These efforts involve leadership enhancement at various levels of the state – from the presidency to local councilors – and the capacities of communities and their leaders and representatives to engage in development priority setting, planning, budgeting, and implementation. Investing in leadership skills throughout society is a critical approach to long-term recovery from conflict. Moreover, improving individual capacities throughout society is an underlying logic in conflict transformation approaches that emphasize the base of leaders' behavior embedded in networks of mid-level leaders, public administrators, civil societies, and citizens. For peace to be enduring, capacities need to be developed simultaneously at all levels in both the state and in society. This complexity of social organization suggests that in the twenty-first century, institutionalizing the peace will also require the development of modern forms of dialogue-based democracy, which place a premium on inclusion, participation, and accountability, and as noted in the conclusion of chapter 5, at the very local level.

The long-term goals of statebuilding in post-civil war settings requires a consistent and determined focus on consolidating peace through a laser-like focus on the institutions of the state. Strengthening the international regime to aid statebuilding will continue to require new approaches and methods for aid delivery that directly improve on the durability, functioning, and resilience of core state institutions: the institutions that govern the security forces and police, the capacity of government bureaucracies to formulate policy, regulate markets, and deliver services at the local level, and the processes of legitimatization grounded in electoral processes, parliaments, and civil society.

In conclusion, statebuilding today is no longer simply about the protection of societies from external threat, the accumulation of power and authority by centralizing elites (whether by coercion or inducement), or creating rationalized structures of bureaucracy to facilitate trade. Now and into the future, statebuilding after civil war will unfold when international interveners seeking to consolidate peace can more effectively augment internal processes of transition and reform in a way that incentivizes local elites to extend their authority through consent not coercion, to improve the capacity to deliver in a way that addresses basic human needs for all, and that grounds their legitimacy in rights-based democratic processes consistent with international obligations, and, increasingly, their own citizens' demands.

Notes

PREFACE

1 The International Crisis Group reported that in the wake of the rebel victory in the civil war:

> The militias that were decisive in ousting Qadhafi's regime are becoming a significant problem now that it is gone. Their number is a mystery: 100 according to some; three times that others say. Over 125,000 Libyans are said to be armed. The groups do not see themselves as serving a central authority; they have separate procedures to register members and weapons, arrest and detain suspects; they repeatedly have clashed.

(International Crisis Group, "Holding Libya Together: Security Challenges after Qadhafi," No. 115, December 14, 2011, p. 1; available at: http://www.crisisgroup.org/en/regions/middle-east-north-africa/north-africa/libya/115-holding-libya-together-security-challenges-after-qadhafi.aspx).

2 Briefing by Mr Ian Martin to the United Nations Security Council, July 18, 2012, available at: http://unsmil.unmissions.org/Default.aspx?tabid=3543&ctl=Details&mid=6187&ItemID=409044&language=en-US.

INTRODUCTION

1 See the July 2009 "Report of the Secretary General on Peacebuilding in the Immediate Aftermath of Conflict" (A/63/881–S/2009/304) (United Nations 2009) and The 2010 National Security Strategy of the United States, at http://www.whitehouse.gov/sites/default/files/rss_viewer/national_security_strategy.pdf.

2 See the World Bank's *Millennium Development Goals Global Monitoring Report 2007: Confronting the Challenges of Gender Equality and Fragile States*, at http://siteresources.worldbank.org/ INTGLOMONREP2007/Resources/3413191-1179404785559/ Overview-GMR07_webPDF-corrected-may-14-2007-2.pdf. See also OECD-DAC, "Ensuring Fragile States are Not Left Behind," March 2009, available at: http://www.oecd.org/dataoecd/34/24/ 40090369.pdf.

3 The definition is included in the normative frameworks developed in the donor community to address engagement in fragile states; see the OECD-DAC "Principles for Good International Engagement in Fragile States and Situations" (Paris Declaration), OECD, Paris, 2007 and the Accra Principles for Good International Engagement in Fragile States and Situations, para. 3, April 2007. Available at http://www.oecd.org/dataoecd/ 61/45/38368714.pdf.

4 See chapter 1 for a discussion of the terminology debates around fragility. The term is sometimes contentious as local elites often protest the "fragile-state" appellation.

5 For an evaluation of the hypothesis that climate change will induce new armed conflicts, see Buhaug et al. (2008).

6 See also Fukuyama, who argues that "The art of statebuilding will be a key component of national power [to the United States], as important as the ability to deploy traditional military force to the maintenance of world order" (2004: 121).

7 As quoted in "Report on Post-Conflict Civilian Capacity Stresses Stronger National Ownership of Peace Processes, Need to Broaden Experts' Pool in Security Council Debate." Security Council SC/10249, May 12, 2011. Available at: http://www.un. org/News/Press/docs//2011/sc10249.doc.htm.

CHAPTER 1 CIVIL WAR AND POST-WAR FRAGILITY

1 In this book, I adopt a broader definition of civil war. There is a debate in the scholarly literature and in policy practice about the term "civil war." In terms of scholarship, "war" often applies to an intense armed conflict that escalates to a certain threshold (typically, 1,000 battle-related fatalities over the lifespan of the conflict) (see the definitions of the Uppsala Conflict Data

Program at http://www.pcr.uu.se/research/ucdp/definitions/).
In policy terms, labeling a conflict a civil war has significant
connotations in terms of state sovereignty and in international
law, for example the application of the laws of war and in terms
of the definition of war crimes and crimes against humanity. The
latter debates played out in 2005 in whether to define sectarian
violence and insurgency in Iraq as a civil war and in early 2012
as United Nations officials struggled with the escalating conflict
in Syria, eventually taking the step of labeling the imbroglio
a civil war. In this book, I refer broadly to civil war to include
armed conflict as defined in the Uppsala Conflict Data Program
definition referenced above.

2 The nomenclature of "new wars" was coined by Mary Kaldor
(1999). Historical precedents for international intervention in
civil wars are seen, for example, in the 1960–64 United Nations
intervention in post-colonial Congo.

3 The conflict between Ethiopia and Eritrea, fought over borders
of the newly formed Eritrean state, is an exception: this war from
1998 to 2000 left up to 100,000 dead in World War I-type trench
warfare.

4 Uppsala Conflict Data Program, Conflict Termination dataset v.
2.0, 1946–2006.

5 See also Hironaka (2005) for an extensive analysis of war
duration. She argues that the principal explanation for longer civil
wars in the contemporary era is their internationalization; she
concludes that "civil wars of the late twentieth century are, to a
certain extent, creatures of the international system. Although the
principal triggers of civil wars are local in origin, the magnitude
and duration of these wars are the product of international
processes and resources" (Hironaka 2005: 149).

6 In a reversal of historical patterns reaching back into the
twentieth century, in which military victory was more likely, in
the period since 1989 more conflicts ended at the negotiating
table than on the battlefield or in the streets. Some, such as Mack
(2007) have argued that the decline in armed conflict in 1992
is causally related to the increased abilities of the international
community (and particularly the UN) to prevent and manage the
effects of conflict and to build peace in civil-war settings. See also
Harbom et al. (2006).

7 "Post-conflict" is a phrase often seen in UN documents. I prefer

not to use this term because of the ubiquity of conflict in the
human condition and the view that conflict as such can be
constructive as well as destructive; "post-war" is a more accurate
term.

8 See Slotin et al. (2010).

9 For an evaluation of whether globalization and trade linkages
have an exacerbating effect on internal conflict, see Schneider et
al. (2003).

10 As Paul Brass writes:

> Every state . . . tends to support particular groups, to distribute
> privileges unequally, and to differentiate among various categories
> in the population . . . The state itself is the greatest prize and
> resource over which groups engage in a continuing struggle in
> societies that have not developed stable relationships among the
> main institutions and centrally organized social forces (1985: 9,
> 29).

11 See Reno (1995) for an analysis of predatory elites in Sierra Leone
and his concept of the "warlord state."

12 For an evaluation, see the report by Amnesty International at
www.amnestyusa.org/diamonds/index.do.

13 The United Nations Environment Program, for example,
has evaluated the impact of land degradation and drought on
migration patterns in the area and has argued that these factors
have been "in large part associated with" the Darfur imbroglio.
See Borger (2007).

14 See Öhman (2005) and Rothchild and Groth (1995) on these
aspects of psychological theories of the origins of difference and
their potential escalation into deadly ethnic violence.

15 The International Crisis Group reported in early 2012 that:

> In some parts of the country, protests are taking on a progressively
> more sectarian tone; a prominent opposition leader in Homs –
> whose family members reportedly were murdered by the regime
> in retaliation for his earlier, more moderate stance – was caught on
> video participating in chants calling to "exterminate the Alawites."
> Sectarian intolerance is everywhere on the rise, and civil strife is
> spreading from central Syria to places like suburban Damascus,
> where a pattern of communal-based killings has been noted. At
> the same time, fundamentalism is becoming more pervasive, as

the conflict turns increasingly desperate and deadly, the outside
world passively looks on, and militant Islamist actors abroad play
a more central role in abetting the opposition ("Syria's Phase of
Radicalization," Crisis Group Middle East Briefing No. 33, April 10,
2012, p. 5. Available at: http://www.crisisgroup.org/~/media/Files/
Middle%20East%20North%20Africa/Iraq%20Syria%20Lebanon/
Syria/b033-syrias-phase-of-radicalisation.pdf).

16 See Horowitz (2003) on the dubious assertion of the right to
   secede as route to realization of the UN Charter's guarantee of
   the right of peoples to self-determination (Article 1.2).
17 See, for example, the Canadian Center for Human Security report
   "Human Security in an Urban Century: Local Challenges, Global
   Perspectives," at www.humansecurity-cities.org.
18 See, for example, the UNDP Oslo Governance Center and
   German Center for International Development, *User's Guide
   on Measuring Fragility* (available at http://www.undp.org/
   oslocentre/docs09/Fragility_Users_Guide_(web).pdf). See
   also the World Bank's *Conflict Analysis Framework* (available
   at: lnweb18.worldbank.org/ESSD/sdvext.nsf/67ByDocName/
   ConflictAnalysis); the USAID Conflict Vulnerability Assessment
   Framework (available at: http://www.usaid.gov/our_work/
   cross-cutting_programs/conflict/publications/docs/CMM_
   ConflAssessFrmwrk_May_05.pdf); and Country Indicators for
   Foreign Policy/Carleton University 2001, Country Indicators for
   Foreign Policy Risk Assessment Template (available at: http://
   www.carleton.ca/cifp/docs/studra1101.pdf). The Governance and
   Social Development Resource Center provides a dedicated guide
   to conflict vulnerability assessment tools and instruments used
   by major international organizations and aid agencies, available
   at: http://www.gsdrc.org/index.cfm?objectid=3133E975-14C2-
   620A-277DFFB9CA069184.
19 See the website of the United Nations High Commissioner
   for Refugees, http://www.unhcr.org for updated data; the
   organization presents an annual report "Refugees by Numbers."
20 The Common Country Assessment (CCA) is produced as a joint
   initiative of the United Nations and the Government of Iraq;
   the CCA precedes a United Nations Development Assistance
   Framework (UNDAF) (Common Country Assessment in Iraq,
   2009, p. 3). The report goes on to define the statebuilding agenda

in Iraq, such as "establishing state legitimacy and accountability through an inclusive and participatory political process, increasing the state's capacity to exert its authority, rule by law, ensure security, and protect citizens' rights; and strengthening state capacity to perform other core functions and to deliver services in a manner that is efficient" (p. 23). The "CCA" is available at: www.iauiraq.org/reports/CCA_Final.pdf\.

21 For further detail on this initiative, see the FAO's strategy at http://www.faoiraq.org/images/word/FOA-MOSMA%20 Joint%20Programming%20Strategy.pdf.

22 According to the *Human Development Report 2009* from UNDP, in 2007 94.8 percent of Liberians were living on below $2 per day, with 83.7 percent living on below $1.25 per day. Additionally, enrolment in education was 57.6 percent and adult literacy rates were only 55.5 percent. See McGovern (2008: 335).

23 United Nations Development Program, *Human Development Report 2009, Liberia*. Available at: http://hdrstats.undp.org/en/ countries/data_sheets/cty_ds_LBR.html.

24 United Nations Development Program, *Human Development Report 2009*. Available at: http://hdr.undp.org/en/reports/global/ hdr2009/.

25 Collier argues that

> the classic process by which effective and accountable states have been forged has not been followed by the many small, low-income countries that suddenly found themselves independent following decolonization. Instead, some of them have structural characteristics which make it extremely difficult for them to supply the public meta-goods of security and accountability without which economic development is liable to be frustrated (2009: 26).

26 "Armed conflict" involves the state versus one or more organized and politically motivated armed groups, where there is direct competition for the state or for territory. The term "armed violence" is used to refer to situations of high social violence (such as criminal or gender-based violence). See the Geneva Declaration. 2008. *The Global Burden of Armed Violence*. http:/ /www.genevadeclaration.org/resources-armed-violence-report. html. See also Tilly (2002).

27 These are the Fund for Peace State Failure Index (www. fundforpeace.org), the work of the Center for Systemic Peace

(www.systemicpeace.org), the Brookings Institution's Index of
State Failure in the Developing World (http://www.brookings.
edu/research/reports/2008/02/weak-states-index), Carleton
University's Country Indicators for Foreign Policy (http://www4.
carleton.ca/cifp/), the University of Maryland's Conflict and
Instability Ledger (http://www.cidcm.umd.edu/pc/), and The
Economist Intelligence Unit's Political Instability Index (http:/
/viewswire.eiu.com/site_info.asp?info_name=social_unrest_
table&page=noads&rf=0).

28 These scholars offer the best bird's-eye view of fragility and
conclude that fragility and "armed conflict" are closely linked.
Succinctly summarizing the fragility syndrome, they write that

> Perhaps the greatest challenge in post-war recovery is the
> oversupply of arms and skilled militants under conditions ripe for
> economic exploitation and the expansion of organized crime. Of
> course, countries bordering on war-torn and war-recovery states
> experience serious diffusion and spillover effects that further
> increase and expand the reach of organized crime, stimulate
> political tensions and corruption, increase local and regional
> insecurity, challenge local authorities, and overwhelm the already
> severely limited provision of crucial social services (Marshall and
> Cole 2011: 10).

29 See, for example, the 2011 Dili Declaration emanating from the
International Dialogue on Peacebuilding and Statebuilding,
discussed in chapter 6 (see p. 157).

30 For a guide to the language of peacebuilding and to statebuilding,
see Chetail (2009).

CHAPTER 2 THE STATE INTO THE TWENTY-FIRST CENTURY

1 For a summary and review of scholarship on state formation and
statebuilding in Europe, see Ertman (2005).

2 Many modern Marxist scholars continue to see the state, and
particularly the ways in which states guarantee property rights
and reflect dominant global economic orthodoxies, as a guarantor
of the global capitalist system (Miliband 1973).

3 Interestingly, Lenin takes on the views of anarchists who believe

the state is illegitimate because it is based on coercion; anarchists see the state as not only undesirable, but actually harmful, and they view the best form of social organization to be voluntary associations based on notions of "free love" and "free thought." For an overview of a variety of perspectives in anarchism, see McLaughlin (2007).

4 The treaty can be found at http://www.cfr.org/sovereignty/montevideo-convention-rights-duties-states/p15897.

5 Although some countries, such as Czechoslovakia, the USSR, or Yugoslavia that have dissolved and split, were once members of the United Nations and states in the international system, the dissolution of the state in these cases was voluntary.

6 On the Kosovo case, see Gëzim Krasniqi, "Citizenship as a Tool of Statebuilding in Kosovo: Status, Rights, and Identity in the New State," The Europeanization of Citizenship in the Successor States of the Former Yugoslavia Working Paper Series No. 10 (2010), University of Edinburgh, at http://www.law.ed.ac.uk/file_download/series/216_citizenship asatool ofstatebuildinginkosovostatusrightsandidentityinthenewstate.pdf.

7 State formation refers to the creation of a sovereign state, usually from formerly independent parts or amalgamation of previous principalities (or "statelets"), whereas statebuilding is about the extension of state capacity of existing or newly formed states.

8 For a careful and succinct review of historical social contract theory, drawing on the works of Hobbes, Locke, Rousseau, and Rawls, see Lessnoff (1990).

9 For a review of current theory and perspectives on minority rights, see Jackson Preece (2006).

10 For the literature on global norms and norm diffusion, see Finnemore and Skikkink (1998), and the deep body of literature that has evolved in recent years in the wake of this seminal work.

11 See *A More Secure World: Our Shared Responsibility*. Report of the High-level Panel on Threats, Challenges, and Change, A/59/565, at http://www.un.org/secureworld/report2.pdf.

CHAPTER 3 INTERNATIONAL ENGAGEMENT FOR
STATEBUILDING AFTER CIVIL WAR

1   See the report "Exit Strategies and Peace Consolidation in
    Statebuilding Operations," Report on Wilton Park Conference
    965, 2009, at http://cis.politics.ox.ac.uk/materials/WP965_
    report.pdf.
2   The Essential Tasks Matrix is available online at www.state.gov/s/
    crs/rls/52959.htm.
3   For a review of some recent literature on US perspectives
    on "nation building," see Brownlee (2007). See also the US
    Army report "Finding the Right Measures for Effectiveness for
    Rebuilding the State of Iraq," May 24, 2005, at http://www.
    dtic.mil/cgi-bin/GetTRDoc?Location=U2&doc=GetTRDoc.
    pdf&AD=ADA463246.
4   For example, the immediate security dividends of demobilization,
    disarmament, and security sector reform must be balanced with
    support for critical state institutions (often, the police). Yet often
    police and security forces are tied to informal actors, and there
    are serious pitfalls relating to equipping and training poorly
    trained police forces. There is also the need to balance support for
    reforming the police with processes of transitional justice.
5   Stephen Stedman calculated that only about 15 percent of civil
    wars between the years 1900 and 1980 ended at the peace table
    (1991). See also Fortna (2004a: 87).
6   For details on the Lebanon case, see the 2008/2009 United
    Nations Development Program National Human Development
    Report, *Lebanon: Toward a Citizen's State*, at http://hdr.undp.
    org/en/reports/national/arabstates/lebanon/NHDR_Lebanon_
    20082009_En.pdf.
7   On the process and outcome of statebuilding in the Palestine
    case, see the report of the Office of the Quartet Representative
    (OQR) Tony Blair, "Report for the Meeting of the Ad Hoc Liaison
    Committee on OQR Action in Support of Palestinian Authority
    State-Building," September 18, 2011 (New York), available at:
    http://blair.3cdn.net/f51fb99a037f9880cb_tnm6bckyb.pdf.
8   On the implications of war-ending terms for post-war
    peacebuilding, see Rothchild (2002); on war termination from a
    rational choice approach, see Mason and Fett (1996).
9   For a review and analysis of "political missions," as opposed to

UN peacekeeping operations, see *Political Missions 2011*, Center for International Cooperation, New York University, available at: http://www.cic.nyu.edu/politicalmissions/index.html.

10 See also Cliffe and Manning (2008).

11 Di John and Putzel argue that political settlements "manifest themselves in the structure of property rights and entitlements, which give some social actors more distributional advantages than others, and in the regulatory structure of the state. These settlements, which can take the form of 'political coalitions', may be the result of a narrow or forced bargain imposed by authoritarian regimes, the outcome of compromises between previously warring parties, or the result of more pluralist bargaining arrangements, as in democratic regimes" (2009: 4).

12 See the Humanitarian Policy Group Report, "Power, Livelihoods and Conflict: Case Studies in Political Economy Analysis for Humanitarian Action" (Collinson 2003).

13 See the Governance and Social Development Resource Center "Helpdesk" Research Report on Political Economy Methodologies, at http://www.gsdrc.org/docs/open/HD498.pdf.

14 See the United Kingdom's Department for International Development Practice Paper, "Political Economy Analysis: How to Note," July 2009, at http://www.odi.org.uk/events/documents/1929-dfid-note-political-economy-analysis.pdf.

CHAPTER 4 AUTHORITY: IMPERATIVES OF SECURITY

1 See the 2007 report of the Canadian Consortium on Human Security, "Human Security for an Urban Century: Local Challenges, Global Perspectives," at http://humansecurity-cities.org.

2 United Nations Department of Peacekeeping Operations, *Capstone Doctrine: United Nations Peacekeeping Operations: Principles and Guidelines* (2008), p. 87. Available at: http://www.peacekeepingbestpractices.unlb.org/pbps/library/capstone_doctrine_eng.pdf.

3 See the analysis by Paul D. Williams, "Enhancing Civil Protection in Peace Operations: Insights from Africa," Africa Center for Strategic Studies Research Paper No. 1, National Defense

University (Washington, DC), September 1, 2010. Available at: http://www.ndu.edu/press/lib/pdf/ACSS-Research-Papers/ ACSS-1.pdf.

4 This strategy was used to some effect in Somalia, however, during Operation Provide Comfort in 1992. For earlier work on the question of policing and peace operations, see Oakley et al. (1999).

5 See Doreen Carvajal, "A Female Approach to Peacekeeping," *New York Times*, March 8, 2010, available at: http://www.nytimes.com/2010/03/06/world/africa/06iht-ffpeace.html?pagewanted=all.

6 Often, depending on the situation, other terms are used such as reinsertion, repatriation, resettlement, or rehabilitation of combatants.

7 For the current IDDRS guidelines, see the UN's DDR Resource Center at http://www.unddr.org/iddrs/framework.php.

8 For further on the Northern Ireland case of internationally verified "decommissioning," see the "Briefing Note on the Decommissioning," Conflict Archive on the Internet, University of Ulster, at http://cain.ulst.ac.uk/events/peace/decommission.htm.

9 On transnational organized crime in a fragile state, see Peter Gastrow, "Termites at Work: Transnational Organized Crime and State Erosion in Kenya," International Peace Institute Policy Paper (September 2011), at http://www.ipinst.org/images/pdfs/ipi_epub-kenya-toc.pdf.

10 For details on the Afghanistan program, see www.anbp.af.undp.org/.

11 For further on the linkages between transitional justice and security sector reform, see Patel et al. (2009).

12 For further on the Burundi case, see Nindorera (2007).

13 See the analysis in Lokuji et al. (2009).

14 See Porch (2003) for a discussion and Dobbins et al. (2009) for full review of the Coalition Provisional Authority.

15 Coalition Provisional Authority Order No. 1, available at http://www.iraqcoalition.org/regulations/20030516_CPAORD_1_De-Ba_athification_of_Iraqi_Society_.pdf

16 For example, see Ricks (2006).

17 For conceptualization of the human security concept, see "Human Security in Theory and Practice," United Nations

Trust Fund for Human Security, United Nations Office of the
Coordinator of Humanitarian Affairs (2009), available at: http://
hdr.undp.org/en/media/HS_Handbook_2009.pdf.

18 For an overview of lessons learned in police reform, see O'Neill
(2005).

19 See the UNDP and United Nations Development Fund for
Women (UNIFEM) report, "Gender Sensitive Police Reform
in Post-Conflict Societies," 2007, at http://www.undp.org/cpr/
documents/gender/Gender_Sensitive_Police_Reform_Policy_
Brief_2007.pdf.

20 See the UNDP Report, "Community Security and Social
Cohesion: Towards a UNDP Approach," March 2010. New York:
UNDP Bureau for Crisis Prevention and Recovery.

21 For a review of the implementation of these mechanisms at the
community-based level, see Odendaal and Olivier (2008).

CHAPTER 5 CAPACITY: CREATING THE
CONDITIONS FOR DEVELOPMENT

1 See Huguette Labelle, "Billions down the Afghan Hole," *New
York Times*, July 6, 2012. For a critical review of aid flows in
Afghanistan, see Suhrke (2009).

2 For discussion of these tensions, see Piiparinen (2007).

3 For further, see the report of the Humanitarian Policy Group,
"UN Integration and Humanitarian Space: An Independent
Study Commissioned by the UN Integration Steering Group" by
Victoria Metcalfe, Alison Giffen, and Samir Elhawary, December
2011, p. 14. Available at http://www.odi.org.uk/resources/docs/
7526.pdf.

4 Global Witness, "Timber, Taylor, Soldier, Spy," June 2005, p.
32; available at: http://reliefweb.int/sites/reliefweb.int/files/
resources/1400286C077E899C49257022000DEEC9-gw-lbr-
15jun.pdf.

5 See the report by Saferworld, "Armed Violence in the Terai,"
August 2011. Available at: http://www.smallarmssurvey.org/
fileadmin/docs/E-Co-Publications/SAS-Saferworld-2011-armed-
violence-in-the-Terai.pdf.

6 See the study sponsored by the German Aid Agency (formerly
GTZ), "Armed Conflict and Trafficking in Women," available

at http://www.ungift.org/doc/knowledgehub/resource-centre/ NGO_GTZ_Armed_conflict_and_trafficking_in_women.pdf.

7   For an overview of the literature on this topic, see Samset (2009).

8   OECD-DAC, "Monitoring the Principles for Good International Engagement in Fragile States and Situations," 2010, p. 23, available at: http://www.oecd.org/dataoecd/18/16/44651689.pdf.

9   See the Danish Institute for International Studies Policy Brief, "Taxation and State-building with a (more) Human Face," October 2008, DIIS Policy Brief: Fragile Situations. Available at: http://www.diis.dk/graphics/publications/briefs2008/pb_2008_ 10_taxation_state-building.pdf. For a scholarly perspective on taxation and statebuilding in developing countries more broadly, see Bräutigam et al. (2008).

10 On the social construction of ethnic identities, see Fearon and Laitin (2000).

11 The program is described in further detail at http://www.iq.undp. org.

12 For further on disaster-risk reduction in conflict-affected settings, see the work of the United Nations Environment Program's "Disasters and Conflicts Program." The goal of the UNEP program is to "use environmental cooperation to transform the risks of conflict over resources into opportunities for peace in war-torn societies, and to integrate environment and natural resources issues within the peacebuilding policies and strategies of the UN." The program overview is posted at: http:// postconflict.unep.ch/publications/UNEP_dc.pdf.

13 See the World Public Sector Report 2010, Reconstructing Public Administration after Conflict, UN Public Administration Program (UN DESA). Available at http://www.unpan.org/ DPADM/ProductsServices/WorldPublicSectorReport/tabid/645/ language/en-US/Default.aspx.

14 See the *Liberia National Capacity Development Strategy*, Monrovia: Government of Liberia, Ministry of Planning and Economic Affairs, at http://www.mopea.gov.lr/doc/NCDS.pdf.

15 For an overview of the design and delivery challenges of education service delivery in fragile states, see the Inter-Agency Network for Education in Emergences at http://www.ineesite. org/.

16 Save the Children, *Last in Line, Last in School 2008: How donors can support education for children affected by conflict and emergencies*

(2008). See this report and the Save the Children resource site on education in conflict-affected countries at: http://www.savethechildren.net/alliance/media/newsdesk/2008-06-03.html.

17 For a bibliography of UN-sponsored reports on women, security and development, see the resource site at UN Security Council Report, http://www.securitycouncilreport.org/site/c.glKWLeMTIsG/b.3959813/k.1753/Women_Peace_and_SecuritybrUN_Documents.htm.

18 The committee's statement is at http://nobelpeaceprize.org/en_GB/laureates/laureates-2011/announce-2011/.

19 For further, see the work of the NGO Working Group on Women, Peace, and Security at www.womenpeacesecurity.org.

20 For the most recent analysis, which evaluates the effects of the post-2008 global financial crisis on the role of women in development, see the 2009 *World Survey on the Role of Women in Development*, "Women's Control over Economic Resources and Access to Financial Resources including Microfinance," United Nations Department of Economic and Social Affairs (UN DESA), ST/ESA/326, at http://www.un.org/womenwatch/daw/public/WorldSurvey2009.pdf. The quotation is from page v.

CHAPTER 6 LEGITIMACY: TOWARD A DEMOCRATIC STATE

1 Principally, the right to democracy is found in the International Covenant on Civil and Political Rights, Article 21. See Rich (2001), for an analysis of democracy norms and state obligations in international law.

2 See Sisk (2009).

3 For a fuller evaluation of this question, see Jarstad and Sisk (2008).

4 See Reilly (2003, 2004) for a discussion.

5 Dahl's work is important in understanding the philosophical basis for varieties of democracy, from more competitive or "polyarchical" systems to those that are based on constraints on the tyranny of the majority and the search consensus and restraint on contestation through the features of power sharing. See Dahl (1989: 225–79).

6 For further on debates over power sharing after civil war and the

relationship to statebuilding and democratization, see Roeder and Rothchild (2005).

7 For example, see the IDEA handbook *Democracy and Deep-Rooted Conflict: Options for Negotiators* (Harris and Reilly 1998).

8 For an online resource base on the constitution-making issues, see constitutionmaking.org. For a guide to constitution-making in post-conflict countries, see the International IDEA guide "Constitution Building after Conflict: External Support to a Sovereign Process" (IDEA Policy Paper, May 2011), at http:// www.idea.int/publications/constitution-building-after-conflict/ index.cfm.

9 The text of the agreement is available at: http://www.usip.org/ files/file/resources/collections/peace_agreements/liberia_ 08182003.pdf. See Annex 3 for the timetable of steps leading up to elections in 2005.

10 See the report "Elections in Post-Conflict Countries: Lessons Learned from Liberia, Sierra Leone, DR Congo, and Kosovo," Report of a ZIF (Center for International Peace Operations)/ KAIPTC (Kofi Annan International Peacekeeping Training Center) Seminar, June 12–14, 2008, Accra, Ghana, available at http://www.zif-berlin.org/fileadmin/uploads/analyse/ dokumente/veroeffentlichungen/ZIF_KAIPTC_Elections_ Report_02_09.pdf.

11 See the 2010 UNDP handbook *Elections and Conflict Prevention: A Guide to Analysis, Planning, and Programming,* available at http:// www.undp.org/publications/Elections_and_Conflict_Prevention. pdf. See also work of International IDEA to develop an election-related violence assessment framework at: http://www.undp.org/ publications/Elections_and_Conflict_Prevention.pdf.

12 For further information on legislative support in post-conflict countries, see the report of the Woodrow Wilson School, Princeton University, "Strengthening Legislatures for Conflict Management in Fragile States," n.d., available at: http://wws. princeton.edu/research/final_reports/wws591b.pdf.

13 The goal of the Guatemala dialogue process was described as the following: "In addition to promoting trust among various political elites, *Visión Guatemala* intended to generate a long-term national agenda – to be shared by all sectors of the society – that would serve as a conducting thread, and support and be supported by the Peace Accords." See the *Visión Guatemala* report, authored by

Elena Díez Pinto, at http://www.democraticdialoguenetwork.org/documents/view.pl?s=1;ss=;t=;f_id=263.

14 See the 2006 Report of the Secretary General, "Uniting our Strengths: Enhancing United Nations Support for the Rule of Law," A/61/636–S/2006/980, December 12, 2006, at http://daccess-dds-ny.un.org/doc/UNDOC/GEN/N06/661/01/PDF/N0666101.pdf?OpenElement.

15 For further on the Liberian case, see James-Allen et al. (2010).

16 See the report of the Office of the High Commissioner for Human Rights, "Rule of Law Tools for Post-Conflict States: Maximizing the Legacy of Hybrid Courts," 2008. Available at: http://www.ohchr.org/Documents/Publications/HybridCourts.pdf.

17 See its work at http://www.aihrc.org.af/english/.

18 On this and other approaches to anti-corruption efforts in fragile states, see Harald Mathisen, "Addressing Corruption in Fragile States: What role for Donors?" Anti-Corruption Resource Center U4 Issue No. 1, Christian Michelsen Institute (Bergen, Norway) (2007), available at: http://www.cmi.no/publications/file/2555-addressing-corruption-in-fragile-states.pdf.

19 On the UN program to support the Iraqi board, see the project document at http://www.iq.undp.org/UploadedFiles/Projects/522c6ce9-0532-4a13-8a36-c57c45cf3fd2.pdf.

20 See the report of the Carnegie Commission on Preventing Deadly Conflict, "A House No Longer Divided: Progress and Prospects for Democratic Peace in South Africa" (Stremlau and Zille 1997).

21 The British Charity Actionaid conducted a survey of Afghan women and found that 72 percent of Afghan women believe their lives are better than ten years ago, with 86 percent fearing a return to the Taliban's abrogation of women's rights. See the report "A Just Peace? The Legacy of War for the Women of Afghanistan," at http://www.actionaid.org.uk/doc_lib/a_just_peace.pdf.

22 "International Criminal Court to Investigate Ivory Coast Violence," October 3, 2011, at http://www.guardian.co.uk/world/2011/oct/03/international-criminal-court-ivory-coast.

23 For the complicated outcome of the nine months of post-election coalition formation negotiations, see the Carnegie Endowment for International Peace's resource site at http:/

/carnegieendowment.org/publications/special/misc/
iraqielections2010/.
24 See the joint publication of International IDEA, UNDP,
the Canadian International Development Agency, and the
Organization of American States, *Democratic Dialogue:
A Handbook for Practitioners* (2007) at http://www.
democraticdialoguenetwork.org/index.pl.

CHAPTER 7 STRENGTHENING THE
INTERNATIONAL STATEBUILDING REGIME

1 The phrase "velvet divorce" was coined to describe the peaceful
break-up of the former Czechoslovakia into the present Czech
Republic and Slovakia. The phrase is a play on the so-called
"velvet revolution" through which the country emerged in
a democratization process from Soviet influence and local
Communist Party rule. Scotland's Scottish National Party
government announced in early 2012 that it intends to hold
a referendum on independence from the United Kingdom in
autumn 2014.
2 In March 2010, Secretary-General Ban Ki-moon appointed a
senior advisory group to further explore civilian capacities in
peace operations. Drawing on the advisory group's analysis,
the Secretary-General acknowledged that building the state in
the immediate aftermath of conflict "is not a technical exercise
. . . Supporting post-conflict national institutions is a high-
risk, political undertaking . . . There are tensions between the
imperatives of starting to build national capacity from day one
and delivering early peace dividends like basic services." See
the Report of the Secretary General, "Civilian Capacity in the
Aftermath of Conflict," A/66/311–S/2011/527, available at http:/
/www.civcapreview.org/LinkClick.aspx?fileticket=stoUsF3Lo
GQ%3d&tabid=3188&language=en-US. The Advisory Group
Report, *Civilian Capacity in the Aftermath of Conflict: Independent
Report of the Senior Advisory Group* (2011) is found at: http://www.
civcapreview.org/LinkClick.aspx?fileticket=K5tZZE99vzs%3d&ta
bid=3188&language=en-US.
3 Report of the Secretary General, *Preventive Diplomacy, Delivering
Results*, August 26, 2011, S/2011/552.

4 On the case for the "democratic governance" perspective, see Brown (2003).

5 See the report "Emerging Donors in International Development Assistance: The China Case," International Development Resource Center, December 2007. Available at: http://www.idrc.ca/EN/Documents/Case-of-China.pdf.

6 W. Pal Sidhu, "Linking Development with Security," livemint.com, July 30, 2012; available at http://www.livemint.com/2012/07/08210215/Linking-development-with-secur.html?atype=tp.

7 For further on the Busan "New Deal" agreements, see the International Peace Institute report "Busan and Beyond: Implementing the 'New Deal' for Fragile States," IPI Issue Brief, July 2012, available at http://www.ipacademy.org/media/pdf/publications/ipi_e_pub_busan_and_beyond.pdf.

8 The Monrovia Roadmap, pp. 2–3, available at http://www.oecd.org/dataoecd/23/24/48345560.pdf.

9 UN DESA Policy Brief No. 7, "Statebuilding in Post-Conflict Countries Requires a Different Approach," September 2007, p. 2.

10 As Huang and Harris note in their study of capacity development challenges in Timor-Leste, "In striking contrast to the ubiquity of the term [capacity building], the literature rarely ventures into a deeper discussion of what capacity building is and how it should be done" (2006: 78).

11 See UN DESA and UNDP, "The Challenges of Restoring Governance in Crisis and Post-Conflict Countries," 7th Global Forum on Reinventing Government: Building Trust in Government, June 26–27, 2007, Vienna, Austria.

12 World Bank, "Building Capacity in Post-Conflict Countries," *Social Development Notes*, Conflict Prevention and Reconstruction, No. 14, December 2003.

13 See UNDG, 2008, *UNDG Capacity Assessment Methodology – User Guide: for National Capacity Development*. http://www.undg.org/docs/8947/UNDG-Capacity-Assessment-User-Guide-Feb-2008-FINAL.doc.

14 See the UNDP, Capacity Development Group, Bureau for Development Policy, *Supporting Capacity Development: The UNDP Approach*, June, 2007: 4, which emphasizes that "leadership is the key factor in responding to and recovering from crisis."

15 See Wolpe and MacDonald (2008) on the leadership approach to building state capacity.

References

Alinova, Luca, Günter Hemrich and Luca Russo. 2007. "Addressing Food Insecurity in Fragile States: Case Studies from the Democratic Republic of the Congo, Somalia and Sudan." ESA Working Paper No. 07-21. Rome: Food and Agriculture Organization of the United Nations.

Anderson, Benedict. 1991. *Imagined Communities: Reflections on the Origin and Spread of Nationalism*. London: Verso.

Avant, Deborah. 2009. "Making Peacemakers Out of Spoilers: International Organizations, Private Military Training, and Statebuilding after War," in Roland Paris and Timothy D. Sisk, eds, *The Dilemmas of Statebuilding: Confronting the Contradictions of Post-war Peace Operations*. Abingdon: Routledge.

Ball, Nicole and Luc Van de Goor. 2006. *Disarmament, Demobilization and Reintegration: Mapping Issues, Dilemmas and Guiding Principles*. The Hague: Clingendael (Netherlands Institute for International Affairs).

Ballentine, K. and J. Sherman, eds. 2003. *The Political Economy of Armed Conflict: Beyond Greed and Grievance*. Boulder, CO: Lynne Rienner.

Barnett Michael. 2011. *Empire of Humanity: A History of Humanitarianism*. Ithaca, NY: Cornell University Press.

Barnett, Michael and Christoph Zuercher. 2009. "The Peacebuilder's Contract: How External Intervention Reinforces Weak Statehood," in Roland Paris and Timothy D. Sisk, eds., *The Dilemmas of Statebuilding: Confronting the Contradictions of Post-War Peace Operations*. Abingdon: Routledge.

Bates, Robert. 2008. *When Things Fell Apart: State Failure in Late-Century Africa*. Cambridge: Cambridge University Press.

Belloni, Roberto. 2007. *State Building and International Intervention in Bosnia*. New York: Routledge.

Belloni, Roberto. 2008. "Civil Society in War-to-Democracy Transitions," in Anna Jarstad and Timothy D. Sisk, eds., *War-to-Democracy*

Transitions: Dilemmas of Peace-building. Cambridge: Cambridge University Press.

Berdal, Mats and David H. Ucko, eds. 2009. *Reintegrating Armed Groups after Conflict: Politics, Violence, and Transition.* Abingdon: Routledge.

Bermeo, Nancy. 2003. "What the Literature Says – and Doesn't Say – About Post-war Democratization," *Global Governance* 9 (2): 159–78.

Bieber, Florian. 2006. *Post-War Bosnia: Ethnic Structure, Inequality and Governance of the Public Sector.* London: Palgrave.

Borger, Julian. 2007. "Darfur Conflict Heralds Era of Wars Triggered by Climate Change, UN Report Warns," *Guardian*, June 22. Available at: http://www.guardian.co.uk/environment/2007/jun/23/sudan.climatechange.

Bose, Sumantra. 2002. *Bosnia after Dayton: Nationalist Partition and International Intervention.* London: Hurst & Company.

Boutros-Ghali, Boutros. 1992. *An Agenda for Peace.* New York: United Nations. Available at: http://www.un.org/Docs/SG/agpeace.html.

Brass, Paul. 1985. *Ethnic Groups and the State.* Beckenham, Kent: Croom Helm.

Bräutigam, Deborah, Odd-Helge Fjeldstad, and Mick Moore, eds. 2008. *Taxation and State-building in Developing Countries: Capacity and Consent.* Cambridge: Cambridge University Press.

Brinkerhoff, Jennifer. 2009. "Diasporas and Conflict Societies: Conflict Entrepreneurs, Competing Interests, or Contributors to Stability and Development?" Paper presented at the conference "Global Effects and Local Dynamics of Intrastate Conflicts," International Workshop, Jerusalem, May 17–19. Available at: http://siteresources.worldbank.org/KFDLP/Resources/461197-1236813885206/Brinkerhoff_diasporas-&-post-conflict_11-09_paper.pdf.

Brinkerhoff, Jennifer. 2010. *The Contribution of Diaspora Return to Post-Conflict and Fragile Countries: Key Findings and Recommendations.* Paris: OECD-DAC. Available at: http://www.oecd.org/dataoecd/31/1/46663447.pdf.

Brown, Graham, Arnim Langer, and Frances Stewart. 2007. "A Typology of Post-Conflict Environments." UNDP Background Paper. Available at: http://www.undp.org/cpr/content/economic_recovery/Background_7.pdf.

Brown, Mark Malloch. 2003. "Democratic Governance: Toward a Framework for Sustainable Peace," *Global Governance* 9: 141–6.

Brownlee, Jason. 2007. "Can America Nation-Build?" *World Politics* 59 (2): 314–40.

Brozka, Michael. 2006. "Introduction: Criteria for Evaluating Post-Conflict Reconstruction and Security Sector Reform in Peace Support Operation," *International Peacekeeping* 13 (1): 1–13.

Buhaug, Hålvard, Nils Petter Gleditsch, and Ole Magnus Theissen. 2008. *Implications of Climate Change for Armed Conflict*. Washington, DC: World Bank Group. Available at: http://siteresources.worldbank.org/.

Call, Charles. 2008. "Conclusion," in Charles T. Call with Vanessa Wyeth, eds., *Building States to Build Peace*. Boulder, CO: Lynne Rienner.

Cammack, Diana. 2007. "The Logic of African Neopatrimonialism: What Role for Donors?" *Development Policy Review* 25: 599–614.

Caplan, Richard. 2005. *International Governance of War-torn Territories: Rule and Reconstruction*. Oxford: Oxford University Press.

Caplan, Richard. 2012. *Exit Strategies and State Building*. Oxford: Oxford University Press.

Caspary, George. 2012. "Practical Steps to Help Countries Overcome the Resource Curse: The Extractive Industries Transparency Initiative," *Global Governance: A Review of Multilateralism and International Organizations* 18 (2): 171–84.

Castillejo, Clare. 2011. "Building a State that Works for Women." FRIDE Working Paper No. 107. Available at: www.fride.org.

Chandler, David. 2006. *Empire in Denial: The Politics of State-building*. London: Pluto Press.

Chesterman, Simon. 2001. "Introduction: Global Norms, Local Contexts," in Simon Chesterman, ed., *Civilians in War*. Boulder, CO: Lynne Rienner.

Chesterman, Simon. 2004. *You, the People: The United Nations, Transitional Administration, and Statebuilding*. Oxford: Oxford University Press.

Chesterman, Simon, Tom Farer, and Timothy D. Sisk. 2001. "Competing Claims: Self-Determination and Security at the United Nations." International Peace Institute (formerly International Peace Academy) Policy Brief. Available at: http://www.ipinst.org/index.php/publication/policy-papers/detail/160-competing-claims-self-determination-and-security-in-the-united-nations.html.

Chesterman, Simon, Michael Ignatieff, and Ramesh Thakur. 2004. *Making States Work: From State Failure to State-Building*, report of the *Making States Work* project, a collaboration of the International Peace Academy, the Carr Center for Human Rights Policy at Harvard

University, and the United Nations University. Available at: http://www.ipacademy.org/Publications/Publications.htm.

Chetail, Vincent, ed. 2009. *Post-Conflict Peacebuilding: A Lexicon*. Oxford: Oxford University Press.

Cincotta, Richard P. 2009. "Demographic Challenges to the State," in N. Tschirgi, M. S. Lund, and F. Mancini, eds., *Security and Development: Searching for Critical Connections*. New York: International Peace Institute & Lynne Reiner, pp. 77–98.

Cincotta, Richard P., Robert Engelman, and Daniele Anastasion. 2003. *The Security Demographic: Population and Civil Conflict after The Cold War*. Washington, DC: Population Action International.

Cliffe, Sarah and Nick Manning. 2008. "Practical Approaches to Building State Institutions," in Charles T. Call with Vanessa Wyeth, eds., *Building States to Build Peace*. Boulder, CO: Lynne Rienner.

Cohen, Craig. 2006. "Measuring Progress in Stabilization and Reconstruction," United States Institute of Peace Stabilization and Reconstruction Series No. 1 (March). Available at: www.usip.org/pubs/specialreports/srs/srs1.html.

Collier, Paul. 2009. "The Political Economy of Fragile States and Implications for European Development Policy," May, Oxford University Department of Economics, p. 26. Available at: http://erd.eui.eu/media/Collier.pdf.

Collier, Paul, V. L. Elliott, Håvard Hegre, Anke Hoeffler, Marta Reynal-Querol, and Nicholas Sambanis. 2003. *Breaking the Conflict Trap: Civil War and Development Policy*. Washington, DC: World Bank and Oxford University Press.

Collier, Paul, Anke Hoeffler and Måns Söderbom. 2008. "Post-Conflict Risks," *Journal of Peace Research* 45 (4): 461–78.

Collinson, Sarah. 2003. "Power, Livelihoods and Conflict: Case Studies in Political Economy Analysis for Humanitarian Action." Overseas Development Institute, Humanitarian Policy Group. Available at: http://www.odi.org.uk/sites/odi.org.uk/files/odi-assets/publications-opinion-files/289.pdf.

Cramer, Christopher. 2002. "*Homo Economicus* Goes to War: Methodological Individualism, Rational Choice and the Political Economy of War," *World Development* 30 (11): 1845–64.

Cramer, Christopher. 2009. "Trajectories of Accumulation through War and Peace," in Roland Paris and Timothy D. Sisk, eds., *The Dilemmas of Statebuilding: Confronting the Contradictions of Post-War Peace Operations*. Abingdon: Routledge.

Crocker, Chester A., Fen Osler Hampson, and Pamela Aall. 2004. *Taming Intractable Conflict: Mediation in the Hardest Cases.* Washington, DC: United States Institute of Peace Press.

Dahl, Robert. 1989. *Democracy and its Critics.* New Haven, CT: Yale University Press.

Deng, Francis Mading. 1995. *War of Visions: Conflict of Identities in the Sudan.* Washington, DC: Brookings Institution Press.

Di John, Jonathan and James Putzel. 2009. "Political Settlements," Governance and Social Development Resource Center Issues Paper. At: http://www.gsdrc.org/docs/open/EIRS7.pdf.

Dobbins, James, Seth G. Jones, Keith Crane, Andrew Rathmell, Brett Steele, Richard Teltschik, and Anga Timilsina. 2005. *The UN's Role in Nation-Building: From the Congo to Iraq.* Santa Monica, CA: Rand Corporation. Available at: www.rand.org/pubs/monographs/2005/RAND_MG304.pdf.

Dobbins, James, Seth G. Jones, Benjamin Rundle, and Siddarth Mohandas. 2009. *Occupying Iraq: A History of the Coalition Provisional Authority.* Santa Monica, CA: Rand Corporation.

Doyle, Michael. 1983. "Kant, Liberal Legacies and Foreign Affairs," *Philosophy and Public Affairs.* Part I, 12 (3): 205–35; Part II, 12 (4): 323–53.

Doyle, Michael W. and Nicholas Sambanis. 2000. "International Peacebuilding: A Theoretical and Quantitative Analysis," *American Political Science Review* 94 (4): 779–802.

du Toit, Pierre. 1995. *Statebuilding and Democracy in Southern Africa: Botswana, Zimbabwe and South Africa.* Washington, DC: United States Institute of Peace Press.

Easton, David. 1965. *A Systems Analysis of Political Life.* New York: Wiley.

Edelstein, David. 2009. "Foreign Military Forces and Statebuilding: The Dilemmas of Providing Security in Post-Conflict Environments," in Roland Paris and Timothy D. Sisk, eds., *The Dilemmas of Statebuilding: Confronting the Contradictions of Post-War Peace Operations.* Abingdon: Routledge.

Enough! 2009. "A Comprehensive Approach to Congo's Conflict Minerals," Strategy Paper. Washington, DC: Enough! Project. Available at: http://www.enoughproject.org/publications/comprehensive-approach-conflict-minerals-strategy-paper.

Ertman, Thomas. 2005. "Formation and Statebuilding in Europe," in Thomas Janoski, ed., *The Handbook of Political Sociology: States,*

Civil Societies, and Globalization. Cambridge: Cambridge University Press.

Evans, Peter B. 1995. *Embedded Autonomy: States and Industrial Transformation.* Princeton, NJ: Princeton University Press.

Fearon, James D. 2006. Testimony to the U.S. House of Representatives, Committee on Government Reform, "Iraq: Democracy or Civil War?" September 15. Available at: http://fsi.stanford.edu/publications/iraq_democracy_or_civil_war.

Fearon, James and David Laitin. 2000. "Review: Violence and the Social Construction of Ethnic Identity," *International Organization* 54 (4): 845–77.

Fearon, James and David Laitin. 2003. "Ethnicity, Insurgency, and Civil War," *American Political Science Review* 97 (1): 75–90.

Fearon, James and David Laitin. 2004. "Neotrusteeship and the Problem of Weak States," *International Security* 28 (4): 5–23.

Fessha, Yonatan Tesfaye. 2008. "Institutional Recognition and Accommodation of Ethnic Diversity. Federalism in Ethiopia and South Africa." Doctor of Law Thesis, University of the Western Cape, June 9, 2008. Available at: http://etd.uwc.ac.za/usrfiles/modules/etd/docs/etd_gen8Srv25Nme4_5952_1262639555.pdf.

Finnemore, Martha and Katherine Skikkink. 1998. "International Norm Dynamics and Political Change," *International Organization* 52 (4): 887–917.

Fischer, Martina. 2006. *Civil Society in Conflict Transformation: Ambivalence, Potentials, and Challenges.* Berlin: Berghof Research Center for Constructive Conflict Management.

Fortna, Virginia Page. 2004a. *Peace Time: Cease-Fire Agreements and the Durability of Peace.* Princeton, NJ: Princeton University Press.

Fortna, Virginia Page. 2004b. "Does Peacekeeping Keep Peace? International Intervention and the Duration of Peace after Civil War," *International Studies Quarterly* 48 (2): 269–92.

Fukuyama, Francis. 2004. *State Building: Governance and World Order in the Twenty-First Century.* Ithaca, NY: Cornell University Press.

Gamba, Virginia. 2006. "Post Agreement Demobilization Disarmament, and Reintegration: Toward a New Approach," in John Darby, ed., *Violence and Reconstruction.* Notre Dame, IN: Notre Dame University Press.

Gates, Scott and Mansood Murshed. 2005. "Spatial-Horizontal Inequality and the Maoist Insurgency in Nepal," *Review of Development Economics* 9 (1): 121–34.

Gberie, Lansana. 2007. "Liberia and Sierra Leone: Civil Wars, 1989–2004," in John Laband, ed., *Daily Lives of Civilians in Wartime Africa: From Slavery Days to Rwandan Genocide.* Westport, CT: Greenwood Press.

Geneva Center for Security Policy. 2010. "Cooperating for Peace: The Challenges and Promises of Partnerships in Peace Operations," Geneva Paper, July 30, 2010. Available at: http://www.gcsp.ch/Conflict-and-Peacebuilding/Recent-Publications/Cooperating-for-Peace.

Geneva Declaration Secretariat. 2008. *Global Burden of Armed Violence 2008.* Geneva: Geneva Declaration Secretariat.

Geneva Declaration Secretariat. 2011. *Geneva Declaration on Armed Violence and Development: Lethal Encounters.* Cambridge: Cambridge University Press.

Ghani, Ashraf and Clare Lockhart. 2008. *Fixing Failed States: A Framework for Rebuilding a Fractured World.* Oxford: Oxford University Press.

Ghani, Ashraf, Clare Lockhart, and Michael Carnahan. 2006. "An Agenda for Statebuilding in the Twenty-First Century," *Fletcher Forum on World Affairs* 30 (1): 101–24.

Ghobarah, Hazem Adam, Paul Huth, and Bruce Russett. 2003. "Civil Wars Kill and Maim People – Long after the Shooting Stops," *American Political Science Review* 97 (2): 189–202.

Giddens, Anthony. 1985. *A Contemporary Critique of Historical Materialism. Vol. 2. The Nation State and Violence.* Cambridge: Polity.

Giddens, Anthony. 1987. *The Nation-State and Violence.* Berkeley, CA: University of California Press.

Goldstone, Richard. 2004. "Justice and Reconciliation in Fragmented Societies," in Andreas Wimmer, Richard J. Goldstone, Donald L. Horowitz, Ulrike Joras, and Conrad Schetter, eds., *Facing Ethnic Conflicts: Toward a New Realism.* Lanham, MD: Rowman and Littlefield.

Green, Elliott D. 2011. "The Political Economy of Nation Formation in Modern Tanzania: Explaining Stability in the Face of Diversity," *Commonwealth and Comparative Politics* 49 (2): 223–44.

Gurr, Ted Robert. 1993. *Minorities at Risk: A Global View of Ethnopolitical Conflicts.* Washington, DC: United States Institute of Peace Press.

Gurr, Ted Robert. 2000. *Peoples versus States: Minorities at Risk in the New Century.* Washington, DC: United States Institute of Peace Press.

Gutierri, Karen and Jessica Piombo, eds. 2007. *Interim Governments: Institutional Bridges to Peace and Democracy?* Washington, DC: United States Institute of Peace Press.

Hänggi, Heiner. 2005. "Conceptualizing Security Sector Reform and Reconstruction," in Alan Bryden and Heiner Hänggi, eds., *Reform and Reconstruction of the Security Sector.* Geneva: Center for the Democratic Control of Armed Forces.

Harbom, Lotta, Stina Högbladh and Peter Wallensteen. 2006. "Armed Conflict and Peace Agreements," *Journal of Peace Research* 43(5): 617–31.

Harris, Peter and Ben Reilly, eds. 1998. *Democracy and Deep-Rooted Conflict: Options for Negotiators.* Stockholm: International IDEA.

Harttgen, Kenneth and Stephan Klasen, 2010. "Fragility and MDG Progress: How useful is the Fragility Concept?" Courant Research Centre: Poverty, Equity and Growth, Discussion Papers 41, Göttingen: Courant Research Centre.

Hartzell, Caroline and Matthew Hoddie. 2007. *Crafting Peace. Power-Sharing Institutions and the Negotiated Settlement of Civil Wars.* University Park, PA: Pennsylvania State University Press.

Hegre, Håvard et al. 2009. "Predicting Armed Conflict 2010–2050." Oslo: Peace Research Institute Oslo paper, July 11, 2009. Available at: http://folk.uio.no/hahegre/Papers/Prediction2010.pdf

Henri Dunant Center for Humanitarian Dialogue. 2010. "Engaging with Armed Groups: Dilemmas and Options for Mediators," *Mediation Practice Series* 2 (October). Available at: http://www. hdcentre.org/files/HDC_MPS2_EN.pdf.

Herbst, Jeffrey. 2000. *States and Power in Africa: Comparative Lessons in Authority and Control.* Princeton, NJ: Princeton University Press.

Hermann, Margaret G. and Herman W. Kegley, Jr. 2001. "Democracies and Intervention: Is There a Danger Zone in the Democratic Peace?" *Journal of Peace Research* 38 (2): 237–45.

Hewitt, J. Joseph, Jonathan Wilkenfeld, and Ted Robert Gurr. 2010. *Peace and Conflict 2010.* College Park, MD: University of Maryland Center for International Development and Conflict Management (CIDCM). Available at: http://www.cidcm.umd.edu/pc/.

Hironaka, Ann. 2005. *Neverending Wars: The International Community, Weak States, and the Perpetuation of Civil War.* Cambridge, MA: Harvard University Press.

Hobsbawn, Eric. 1983. "Introduction: Inventing Traditions, and 'Mass-Producing' Traditions: Europe, 1870–1914," in Eric Hobsbawn and Terence Ranger, eds., *The Invention of Tradition*. Cambridge: Cambridge University Press.

Hoeffler, Anke and Mara Reynal-Querol. 2003. "Measuring the Costs of Conflict," Centre for the Study of African Economies, University of Oxford. Available at: http://heisun1.unige.ch/sas/files/portal/issueareas/victims/Victims_pdf/2003_Hoeffler_Reynal.pdf.

Höglund, Kristine. 2008. "Violence in War-to-Democracy Transitions," in Anna Jarstad and Timothy D. Sisk, eds., *From War to Democracy: Dilemmas of Peacebuilding*. Cambridge: Cambridge University Press.

Holbrooke, Richard. 1999. *To End a War*. New York: Modern Library.

Horn, Adrian, 'Funmi Olonisakin, and Gordon Peake. 2006. "United Kingdom-led Security Sector Reform in Sierra Leone," *Civil Wars* 8 (2): 109–23.

Horowitz, Donald. 1985. *Ethnic Groups in Conflict*. Berkeley, CA: University of California Press.

Horowitz, Donald. 2001. *The Deadly Ethnic Riot*. Berkeley, CA: University of California Press.

Horowitz, Donald. 2003. "The Cracked Foundations of the Right to Secede," *Journal of Democracy* 14 (2): 5–17.

Huang, Reydo and Joseph Harris. 2006. "The Nuts and Bolts of Post-Conflict Capacity Building," *Journal of Peacebuilding and Development* 2 (3): 78–92.

Hudson, Valerie M., Mary Caprioli, Bonnie Ballif-Spanvill, Rose McDermott, and Chad F. Emmett. 2009. "The Heart of the Matter: The Security of Women and the Security of States," *International Security* 33 (3): 7–45.

Hughes, Barry, Jonathan Moyer, and Timothy Sisk. 2011. "Vulnerability to Intrastate Conflict: Evaluating Quantitative Measures," Washington, D.C.: United States Institute of Peace *Peaceworks*, No. 72 (June 2011). Available at: http://www.usip.org/files/resources/Vulnerability_to_Intrastate_Conflict.pdf

Hyden, Goran. 1999. "Governance and the Reconstitution of Political Order," in Richard Joseph, ed., *State, Conflict, and Democracy in Africa*. Boulder, CO: Lynne Rienner.

International Commission on State Sovereignty (ICSS). 2001. *The Responsibility to Protect*. Ottawa: International Development Research Center. Available at: http://responsibilitytoprotect.org/ICISS%20Report.pdf

International Institute for Democracy and Election Assistance. 2009. *Transitional Justice and Reconciliation after Violent Conflict: Learning from African Experiences.* Stockholm: International IDEA. Available at: http://www.idea.int/conflict/trad_justice_mechanisms.cfm.

International Peace Institute (formerly, International Peace Academy). 2009. *Peace Operations: IPI Blue Paper no. 9.* New York: International Peace Institute.

Jackson Preece, Jennifer. 2006. *Minority Rights.* Cambridge: Polity.

James-Allen, Paul, Aaron Weah, and Lizzie Goodfriend. 2010. *Beyond the Truth and Reconciliation Commission: Transitional Justice Options in Liberia.* New York: International Center for Transitional Justice.

Jarstad, Anna and Timothy D. Sisk, eds. 2008. *From War to Democracy: Dilemmas of Peacebuilding.* Cambridge: Cambridge University Press.

Jenkins, J. Craig and Ester E. Gottlieb. 2007. "Identity Conflicts and their Regulation: An Introduction," and "Can Violence be Regulated?" in J. Craig Jenkins and Ester E. Gottlieb, eds., *Identity Conflicts: Can Violence be Regulated?* New Brunswick, NJ: Transaction Publishers.

Jennings, Kathleen. 2008. "Unclear Ends, Unclear Means: Reintegration in Postwar Societies – The Case of Liberia," *Global Governance* 14 (3): 327–45.

Kalder, Mary. 1999. *New and Old Wars: Organized Violence in a Global Era.* Cambridge: Polity.

Kaufman, Stuart J. 2001. *Modern Hatreds: The Symbolic Politics of Ethnic War.* Ithaca, NY: Cornell University Press.

Krasner, Stephen. 1984. "Approaches to the State: Alternative Conceptions and Historical Dynamics," *Comparative Politics* 16 (January): 223–46.

Krasner, Stephen. 2004. "Sharing Sovereignty: New Institutions for Collapsed and Failing States," *International Security* 29 (2): 85–120.

Krasner, Stephen D. and Carlos Pascual. 2005. "Addressing State Failure," *Foreign Affairs* (July/August). Available at: http://www.foreignaffairs.com/articles/60832/stephen-d-krasner-and-carlos-pascual/addressing-state-failure

Kurtenbach, Sabine. 2008. "Youth Violence in Post-War Societies: Conceptual Considerations on Continuity and Change in Violence." Project Working Paper No. 1, Social and Political Fractures after War, German Foundation for Peace Research. Available at: http://www.postwar-violence.de/files/wp1_concept_postwar_youth_violence.pdf/.

Kurtenbach, Sabine. 2011. "State-building, War and Violence: Evidence from Latin America." German Institute for Global and Area Studies (GIGA) Working Paper No. 181. Hamburg: GIGA.

Lake, David A. 2013. "US Approaches to Statebuilding in Iraq," in David Chandler and Timothy D. Sisk, eds., *The Handbook of International Statebuilding*. Abingdon: Routledge.

Lake, David A. and Donald Rothchild. 1996. "Containing Fear: The Origins and Management of Ethnic Conflict," *International Security* 21 (2): 41–75.

Larémont, Ricardo Rene, ed. 2005. *Borders, Nationalism and the African State*. Boulder, CO: Lynne Rienner.

Large, Judith and Timothy D. Sisk. 2006. *Democracy, Conflict and Human Security: Pursuing Peace in the 21st Century*. Stockholm: International IDEA.

Lemarchand, René. 2006. "Consociationalism and Power Sharing in Africa: Rwanda, Burundi, and the Democratic Republic of Congo," *African Affairs* 106/422: 1–20.

Lenin, Vladimir. 2009 [1918]. *The State and Revolution*. London: Penguin.

Lessnoff, Michael Harry, ed. 1990. *Social Contract Theory*. Oxford: Basil Blackwell.

Licklider, Roy. 1995. "The Consequences of Negotiated Settlements in Civil Wars, 1945–1993," *American Political Science Review* 89 (3): 681–90.

Lijphart, Arend. 2004. "Constitutional Design for Divided Societies," *Journal of Democracy* 15 (2): 96–109.

Linz, Juan. 1993. "Statebuilding and Nation Building," *European Review* 1 (4): 355–69.

Lokuji, Alfred Sebit, Afbraham Sewonet Abatneh, and Chaplain Kenyi Wani. 2009. "Police Reform in Southern Sudan," The North-South Institute Policy Document. Ottawa: The North-South Institute.

Lyons, Terrence. 2005. *Demilitarizing Politics: Elections on the Uncertain Road between War and Peace*. Boulder, CO: Lynne Rienner.

McFate, Sean. 2010. "The Link between DDR and SSR in Conflict-Affected Countries," United States Institute of Peace Special Report. Washington, DC: United States Institute of Peace. Available at: http://reliefweb.int/sites/reliefweb.int/files/reliefweb_pdf/brief-ingkit-e9e334ecacf92d9b22fdb36228a486d9.pdf.

MacGinty, Roger. 2010. "Hybrid Peace: The Interaction between Top-Down and Bottom-Up Peace," *Security Dialogue* 41 (4): 391–412.

McGovern, Mike. 2008. "Liberia: The Risks of Rebuilding a Shadow State," in Charles T. Call with Vanessa Wyeth, eds., *Building States to Build Peace*. Boulder, CO: Lynne Rienner.

McLaughlin, Paul. 2007. *Anarchism and Authority: A Philosophical Introduction to Classical Anarchism*. Cambridge, MA: Blackwell Publishers.

Mack, Andrew. 2007. *Human Security Brief 2007*. Vancouver: Human Security Centre, University of British Columbia. Available at: www.humansecuritybrief.info/.

March, James G. and Johan P. Olsen. 1984. "The New Institutionalism: Organizational Factors in Political Life," *The American Political Science Review* 78: 734–79.

Marshall, Monty G. and Benjamin R. Cole. 2011. *Global Report 2011: Conflict, Governance, and State Fragility*. Center for Systemic Peace, George Mason University. Available at: http://www.systemicpeace.org/GlobalReport2011.pdf.

Marx, Karl and Friedrich Engels. 2006. *Communist Manifesto*. New York: Socialist Labor Party of America.

Mason, T. David and Patrick J. Fett. 1996. "How Civil Wars End: A Rational Choice Approach," *Journal of Conflict Resolution* 40: 546–68.

Migdal, Joel. 1988. *Strong Societies and Weak States: State-Society Relations and State Capabilities in the Third World*. Princeton, NJ: Princeton University Press.

Migdal, Joel. 2001. *State in Society: Studying How States and Societies Transform and Constitute One Another*. Cambridge: Cambridge University Press.

Migdal, Joel, Atul Kohli, and Vivienne Shue, eds. 1994. *State Power and Social Forces: Domination and Transformation in the Third World*. Cambridge: Cambridge University Press.

Miliband, Ralph. 1973. *The State in Capitalist Society*. London: Quartet Books.

Mommsen, Wolfgang J. 1992. *The Political and Social Theory of Max Weber: Collected Essays*. Chicago, IL: University of Chicago Press.

Moore, Mick and James Putzel. 1999. *Thinking Strategically about Politics and Poverty*. Brighton: Institute of Development Studies.

Muggah, Robert, ed. 2009. *Security and Post-Conflict Reconstruction: Dealing with Fighters in the Aftermath of War*. Abingdon: Routledge.

Muggah, Robert and Keith Krause. 2009. "Closing the Gap between Peace Operations and Post-Conflict Insecurity: Towards a Violence Reduction Agenda," *International Peacekeeping* 16 (1): 136–50.

Newman, Edward. 2009. "'Liberal Peacebuilding Debates," in Edward Newman, Roland Paris, and Oliver P. Richmond, eds., *New Perspectives on Liberal Peacebuilding*. Tokyo: United Nations University Press.

Newman, Edward, Roland Paris, and Oliver P. Richmond, eds. 2009. *New Perspectives on Liberal Peacebuilding.* Tokyo: United Nations University Press.

Nindorera, Willy. 2007. "Security Sector Reform in Burundi: Issues and Challenges for Improving Civilian Protection," CENAP/NSI Working Paper, Centre d'Alerte et de Prévention des Conflits (CENAP), Bujumbura, and The North-South Institute, Ottawa.

Oakley, Robert B., Michael J. Dziedzic, and Eliot M. Goldberg. 1999. *Policing the New World Disorder: Peace Operations and Public Security.* Washington DC: Institute for National Security Studies, National Defense University. Available at: www.ndu.edu/inss/books/.

Odendaal, Andries and Retief Olivier. 2008. "Local Peace Committees: Some Reflections and Lessons Learned," Report Commissioned by the Academy for Educational Development. Washington, DC: Academy for Educational Development. Available at: http://unpan1.un.org/intradoc/groups/public/documents/UN/UNPAN032148.pdf.

OECD-DAC (Organization for Economic Development and Cooperation, Development Assistance Committee). 2007. *OECD Handbook on Security Sector Reform.* Paris: OECD. Available at: http://www.oecd.org/development/conflictandfragility/38406485.pdf.

OECD-DAC. 2008. *Concepts and Dilemmas of State Building in Fragile States.* Paris: OECD. Available at: http://www.oecd.org/dac/conflictandfragility/conceptsanddilemmasofstatebuildinginfragilesituationsfromfragilitytoresilience.htm.

OECD-DAC. 2009. *Armed Violence Reduction: Enabling Development.* Paris: OECD. Available at: http://www.oecd.org/dac/conflictandfragility/armedviolencereductionenablingdevelopment.htm.

OECD-DAC. 2010a. *Do No Harm: International Support for Statebuilding.* Paris: OECD. Available at: http://www.oecd.org/dac/conflictandfragility/donoharminternationalsupportforstatebuilding.htm

OECD-DAC. 2010b. International Network on Conflict and Fragility. *The State's Legitimacy in Fragile Situations.* Paris: OECD. Available at: http://www.oecd.org/dac/thestateslegitimacyinfragilesituations.htm.

Öhman, Arne 2005. "Conditioned Fear of a Face: A Prelude to Ethnic Enmity?" *Science* 39 (5735): 711–13.

Olson, Mancur. 2000. *Power and Prosperity.* New York: Basic Books.

O'Neill, William G. 2005. "Police Reform in Post-Conflict Societies: What We Know and What We Still Need to Know," International Peace Academy Policy Paper. New York: International Peace Institute (formerly, International Peace Academy). Available at: http://unddr. org/docs/police_reform_post-conflict.pdf.

Orwell, George. 1968 [1945]. "The Sporting Spirit," in Sonia Orwell and Ian Angus, *In Front of Your Nose: The Collected Essays, Journalism and Letters of George Orwell (Volume IV, 1945–1950)*. New York: Harcourt, Brace & World.

Ostrom, Elinor. 1996. "Cross the Great Divide: Coproduction, Synergy, and Development," *World Development* 24 (6): 1073–87.

Özerdem, Alpaslan. 2009. *Post-War Recovery: Disarmament, Demobilization, and Reintegration*. London: I. B. Taurus.

Paffenholz, Thania, and Christoph Spurk. 2006. "Civil Society, Civic Engagement, and Peacebuilding," World Bank Social Development Papers: Conflict Prevention and Reconstruction (Paper No. 36). Washington, DC: World Bank. Available at: http://siteresources. worldbank.org/INTCPR/Resources/WP36_web.pdf.

Paris, Roland. 2002. "International Peacebuilding and the 'Mission Civilisatrice'," *Review of International Studies* 28 (4). 637–56.

Paris, Roland. 2004. *At War's End: Building Peace after Civil Conflict*. Cambridge: Cambridge University Press.

Paris, Roland. 2009. "Understanding the 'Coordination Problem' in Postwar Statebuilding," in Roland Paris and Timothy D. Sisk, eds., *The Dilemmas of Statebuilding: Confronting the Contradictions of Postwar Peace Operations*. Abingdon: Routledge.

Paris, Roland and Timothy D. Sisk, eds. 2009. *The Dilemmas of Statebuilding: Confronting the Contradictions of Postwar Peace Operations*. Abingdon: Routledge.

Patel, Ana Cutter, Pablo de Greiff, and Lars Waldorf. 2009. *Disarming the Past: Transitional Justice and Ex-Combatants*. New York: Social Science Research Council. Available at: http://www.ssrc.org/work-space/images/crm/new_publication_3/%7B465ede38-0c0d-df11-9d 32-001cc477ec70%7D.pdf.

Patrick, Stewart. 2011. *Weak Links: Fragile States, Global Threats, and International Security*. Oxford. Oxford University Press.

Piiparinen, Touko. 2007. "A Clash of Mindsets? An Insider's Account of Provincial Reconstruction Teams," *International Peacekeeping* 14 (1): 143–57.

Porch, Douglas. 2003. "Strategic Insight: Germany, Japan, and the De-Baathification of Iraq," Monterey, CA: Center for Contemporary Conflict, Naval Post-Graduate School. Available at: http://www.dtic.

mil/cgi-bin/GetTRDoc?AD=ADA485192&Location=U2&doc=GetT RDoc.pdf.

Porto, João Gomes, Chris Alden, and Imogen Parsons. 2007. *From Soldiers to Citizens: Demilitarization of Conflict and Society*. Aldershot: Ashgate Publishing.

Putnam, Robert D. with Robert Leonard and Rafaella Y. Nanetti. 1994. *Making Democracy Work: Civic Traditions in Modern Italy*. Princeton, NJ: Princeton University Press.

Reilly, Benjamin. 2003. "Democratic Validation," in John Darby and Roger MacGinty, eds., *Contemporary Peacemaking: Conflict, Violence and Peace Processes*. London: Palgrave.

Reilly, Benjamin. 2004. "Elections in Post-Conflict Societies," in Edward Newman and Roland Rich, eds., *The UN Role in Promoting Democracy: Between Ideals and Reality*. Tokyo: United Nations University Press.

Reilly, Benjamin and Per Norlund. 2008. *Political Parties in Conflict-Prone Societies: Regulation, Engineering, and Democratic Development*. Tokyo: United Nations University Press.

Reinicke, Wolfgang H., Francis Deng, Jan Martin Witte, Thorsten Benner, Beth Whitaker, and John Gershmann. 2001. *Critical Choices: The United Nations, Networks, and the Future of Governance*. Ottawa: International Development Research Center.

Reno, William. 1995. *Corruption and State Politics in Sierra Leone*. Cambridge: Cambridge University Press.

Rich, Roland. 2001. "Bringing Democracy into International Law," *Journal of Democracy* 12 (3): 20–34.

Ricks, Thomas E. 2006. *Fiasco: The American Military Adventure in Iraq*. New York: Penguin.

Rocha Menocal, Alina. 2009. "State-building for Peace: A New Paradigm for International Engagement in Post-Conflict Fragile States?" Workshop paper for the European Report on Development. Available at: http://www.gsdrc.org/go/display&type=Document&id=3914.

Roeder, Phillip and Donald Rothchild, eds. 2005. *Sustainable Peace: Power and Democracy after Civil War*. Ithaca, NY: Cornell University Press.

Ross, Michael. 2004. "How Does Natural Resource Wealth Influence Civil Wars?" *International Organization* 58 (1): 35–67.

Rotberg, Robert, ed. 2003. *When States Fail: Causes and Consequences*. Princeton, NJ: Princeton University Press.

Rothchild, Donald. 2002. "Settlement Terms and Post-Agreement Stability," in Stephen J. Stedman, Donald Rothchild, and Elizabeth

M. Cousens, eds., *Ending Civil Wars: The Implementation of Peace Agreements*. Boulder, CO: Lynne Rienner.

Rothchild, Donald and Alexander L. Groth. 1995. "Pathological Dimensions of Domestic and International Ethnicity," *Political Science Quarterly* 110 (1): 69–82.

Rubin, Barnett. 2003. *Blood on the Doorstep: The Politics of Preventive Action*. New York: Council on Foreign Relations.

Rubin, Barnett. 2008. "The Politics of Security in Post-Conflict Statebuilding," in Charles T. Call with Vanessa Wyeth, eds., *Building States to Build Peace*. Boulder, CO: Lynne Rienner.

Salahub, Jennifer Erin. 2011. "Hearing from Women on Both Sides of the Thin Blue Line," in Jennifer Erin Salahub, ed., *African Women on the Thin Blue Line*. Ottawa: The North-South Institute.

Sambanis, Nicholas. 2000. "Partition as a Solution to Ethnic War: An Empirical Critique of the Theoretical Literature," *World Politics* 52 (4): 437–83.

Samset, Ingrid. 2009. "Natural Resource Wealth, Conflict, and Peacebuilding." New York: Program on States and Security, Ralph Bunche Institute for International Studies, The Graduate Center at the City University of New York. Available at: http://www.cmi.no/ publications/file/3283-natural-resource-wealth-conflict.pdf.

Sandole, Dennis J. D. 2011. *Peacebuilding*. Cambridge: Polity Press.

Sartori, Giovanni. 1968. "Political Development and Political Engineering," in John D. Montgomery and Albert O. Hirschman, eds., *Public Policy, Vol. XVII*. Cambridge, MA: Harvard University Press.

Schedler, Andreas. 1999. "Restraining the State: Conflicts and Agents of Accountability," in Andreas Schedler, Larry Diamond, and Marc F. Plattner, eds., *The Self-Restraining State: Power and Accountability in New Democracies*. Boulder, CO: Lynne Rienner.

Schneider, Gerald, Katherine Barbeieri, and Nils Petter Gleditsch. 2003. *Globalization and Armed Conflict*. Lanham, MD: Rowman and Littlefield.

Scott, James C. 1999. *Seeing Like a State: How Certain Schemes to Improve the Human Condition Have Failed*. New Haven, CT: Yale University Press.

Sen, Amartya. 1999. "Democracy as a Universal Value," *Journal of Democracy* 10 (3): 3–17.

Shankleman, Jill. 2011. "Mitigating Risks and Realizing Opportunities: Environmental and Social Standards for Foreign Direct Investment in High-value Natural Resources," in Päivi Lujala and Siri Aas Rustad, eds., *High-Value Natural Resources and Post-Conflict Peacebuilding*. Abingdon: Earthscan.

Simmons, P. J. and Chantal de Jonge Oudraat, eds. 2001. *Managing Global Issues: Lessons Learned*. Washington, DC: Carnegie Endowment for International Peace.

Sisk, Timothy D. 2008. "Peacebuilding as Democratization: Findings and Implications," in Anna Jarstad and Timothy D. Sisk, eds., *From War to Democracy: Dilemmas of Peacebuilding*. Cambridge: Cambridge University Press.

Sisk, Timothy D. 2009. "Pathway of the Political: Electoral Processes and Statebuilding after Civil War," in Roland Paris and Timothy D. Sisk, eds., *The Dilemmas of Statebuilding: Confronting the Contradictions of Postwar Peace Operations*. Abingdon: Routledge.

Skocpol, Theda. 1985. "Bringing the State Back In: Strategies of Analysis in Current Research," in Peter B. Evans, Dietrich Rueschemeyer and Theda Skocpol, eds., *Bringing the State Back In*. Cambridge: Cambridge University Press.

Slotin, Jenna, Vanessa Wyeth, and Paul Romita. 2010. "Power, Politics, and Change: How International Actors Assess Local Context," International Peace Institute. Available at: http://www.ipinst.org/publication/policy-papers/detail/294-power-politics-and-change-how-international-actors-assess-local-context.html.

Small Arms Survey (Graduate Institute of International Studies, Geneva). 2003. *Small Arms Survey 2003: Development Denied*. Oxford: Oxford University Press.

Snyder, Jack. 2000. *From Voting to Violence: Democratization and Nationalist Conflict*. New York: W. W. Norton.

Snyder, Jack and Robert Jervis. 1999. "Civil War and the Security Dilemma," in Barbara Walter and Jack Snyder, eds., *Civil Wars, Insecurity, and Intervention*. New York: Columbia University Press.

Söderberg Kovacs, Mimmi. 2008. "When Rebels Change their Stripes: Armed Insurgents in Post-War Politics," in Anna Jarstad and Timothy D. Sisk, eds., *From War to Democracy: Dilemmas of Peacebuilding*. Cambridge: Cambridge University Press.

Spear, Joanna. 2006. "From Political Economies of War to Political Economies of Peace: The Contribution of DDR after Wars of Predation," *Contemporary Security Policy* 27 (1): 168–89.

Specker, Leontine. 2008. "The R-phase of DDR Processes: An Overview of Key Lessons Learned and Practical Experiences," Conflict Research

Unit, Netherlands Institute for International Relations, Clingendael, September.

Spruyt, Hendrik. 2009. "War, Trade, and State Formation," in Susan C. Stokes and Charles Boix, eds., *The Oxford Handbook of Comparative Politics*. Oxford: Oxford University Press.

Stedman, Stephen. 1991. *Peacemaking in Civil War: International Mediation in Zimbabwe, 1974–1980*. Boulder, CO: Lynne Rienner.

Stewart, Frances J. 2008. *Horizontal Inequalities and Conflict: Understanding Group Conflict in Multiethnic Societies*. Basingstoke: Palgrave Macmillan.

Stewart, Frances. n.d. "Horizontal Inequalities: A Neglected Dimension of Development," Queen Elizabeth House Working Paper Series No. 81. London: Oxford University, Queen Elizabeth House. Available at: http://www3.qeh.ox.ac.uk/pdf/qehwp/qehwps81.pdf.

Stewart, Frances and Graham Brown. 2009. "Fragile States," CRISE Working Paper No. 51. London: Centre for Research on Inequality, Human Security and Ethnicity (CRISE).

Stremlau, John J. and Helen Zille. 1997. *A House No Longer Divided: Progress and Prospects for a Democratic Peace in South Africa*. New York: Carnegie Commission on Preventing Deadly Conflict, Carnegie Corporation of New York.

Suhrke, Astri. 2007. "Dependent State: The Case of Afghanistan." FRIDE Working Paper No. 51. Madrid: FRIDE.

Suhrke, Astri. 2009. "The Dangers of a Tight Embrace: Externally Assisted Statebuilding in Afghanistan," in Roland Paris and Timothy D. Sisk, eds., *The Dilemmas of Statebuilding: Confronting the Contradictions of Postwar Peace Operations*. Abingdon: Routledge.

Suhrke, Astri. 2011. "Virtues of a Narrow Mission: The UN Peace Operation in Nepal," *Global Governance* 17 (1): 37–55.

Swarbrick, Peter, 2006. "Alphabet Soup in the Great Lakes Region: DDR, DDRRR, DCR, SSR, MDRP, CIDDR, CGFDR and CONADER in the DRC," in *Pursuing Security in the Post-Conflict Phase: Implications for Current and Future Peace Operations*. Report on a Workshop held at the Geneva Centre for Security Policy. Geneva: Centre for Security Policy, pp. 27–33.

Themnér, Lotta and Peter Wallensteen. 2011. "Armed Conflicts, 1946–2010." *Journal of Peace Research* 48: 509–23.

Tilly, Charles, 1975. "Western-State Making and Theories of Political Transformation," in Charles Tilly, ed., *The Formation of National States in Western Europe*. Princeton, NJ: Princeton University Press.

Tilly, Charles, 1985. "War Making and State Making as Organized Crime," in Peter Evans, Dietrich Rueschemeyer, and Theda Skocpol, eds., *Bringing the State Back In*. Cambridge: Cambridge University Press.

Tilly, Charles. 1990. *Coercion, Capital, and European States, AD 990–1990*. Oxford: Basil Blackwell.

Tilly, Charles. 2002. "Violence, Terror, and Politics as Usual," *Boston Review* 27 (3): 21–4. Available at: http://www.bostonreview.net/BR27.3/tilly.html.

Toft, Monica Duffy. 2010. "Ending Civil Wars: A Case for Rebel Victory?" *International Security* 34 (4): 7–36.

Tschirgi, Neclâ, Michael S. Lund, and Francesco Mancini, eds. 2010. *Security and Development: Searching for Critical Connections*. Boulder, CO: Lynne Rienner.

Umar, Muhammad Sani. 2007. "Weak States and Democratization: Ethnic and Religious Conflicts in Nigeria," in J. Craig Jenkins and Esther E. Gottlieb, eds., *Identity Conflicts: Can Violence be Regulated?* New Brunswick, NJ: Transactions Publishers.

United Nations. 2009. Report of the Secretary-General on peacebuilding in the immediate aftermath of conflict (A/63/881–S/2009/304).

United Nations Department of Economic and Social Affairs. 2007. *The Challenges of Restoring Governance in Crisis and Post-Conflict Countries*, United Nations Department of Economic and Social Affairs (DESA) and UNDP, 7th Global Forum on Reinventing Government, June 26–29, 2007, Vienna, Austria.

United Nations Department of Peace Operations and Department of Field Support. 2008. *United Nations Peacekeeping: Principles and Guidelines*. Available at: http://www.peacekeepingbestpractices. unlb.org/pbps/library/capstone_doctrine_eng.pdf.

United Nations Department of Peacekeeping Operations. 2009. *A New Partnership Agenda: Creating a New Horizon for Peacekeeping*. Department of Peacekeeping Operation's non-paper. Available at: http://www.un.org/Depts/dpko/dpko/newhorizon.pdf.

United Nations Development Program. 2004. *Practical Guide to Multilateral Needs Assessment in Post-Conflict Countries*. New York: UNDP. Available at: http://www.undp.org/cpr/documents/prevention/integrate/Post_Conflict_Needs_Assessment_methodology.pdf

United Nations Development Program. 2008. *Post-War Economic Recovery: Enabling Local Ingenuity*. New York: UNDP. Available at: http://www.undp.org/cpr/we_do/eco_recovery.shtml.

United Nations Development Program. 2012. *Governance for Peace: Securing the Social Contract.* New York: United Nations Development Program Bureau for Crisis Prevention and Recovery.

United Nations Development Program and the German Center for International Development. 2009. *User's Guide on Measuring Fragility.* New York: UNDP. Available at: http://www.undp.org/oslocentre/docs09/Fragility_Users_Guide_(web).pdf.

United Nations Environment Program. 2004. *Understanding Environment, Conflict and Cooperation.* Geneva: United Nations Environment Program. Available at: http://www.wilsoncenter.org/topics/pubs/unep.pdf.

Unsworth, Sue. 2010. "An Upside-Down View of Governance," Brighton: Institute of Development Studies. Available at www.gsdrc.org/go/display&type=Document&id=1994.

USAID and the BASICS Project. 2006. "Health Service Delivery in Early Recovery Fragile States: Lessons from Afghanistan, Cambodia, Mozambique, and Timor Leste," May. Available at: http://www.basics.org/documents/Early_Recovery_Fragile_States_Zivetz_Final.pdf.

Van der Merwe, Hugo, Victoria Baxter, and Audrey R. Chapman. 2009. *Assessing the Impact of Transitional Justice: Challenges for Empirical Research.* Washington, DC: United States Institute of Peace Press.

Vandewalle, Dirk 2006. *A History of Modern Libya.* Cambridge: Cambridge University Press.

Varshney, Ashutosh. 2001. "Ethnic Conflict and Civil Society: India and Beyond," *World Politics* 53 (3): 362–98.

Vu, Tuong. 2010. "Studying the State through State Formation," *World Politics* 62 (1): 148–75.

Wallensteen, Peter and Margareta Sollenberg. 1998. "Armed Conflict and Regional Conflict Complexes, 1989–1997," *Journal of Peace Research* 35 (5): 621–34.

Walter, Barbara. 1997. "The Critical Barrier to Civil War Settlement," *International Organization* 51 (3): 335–64.

Wantchekon, Leonard. 2004. "The Paradox of 'Warlord' Democracy: A Theoretical Investigation," *American Political Science Review* 98 (1): 17–33.

Weber, Max. 1921. *"Politik als Beruf* [Politics as Vocation]," in *Gesammelte Politische Schriften.* Munich. A translation is available at: http://media.pfeiffer.edu/lridener/dss/Weber/polvoc.html.

Weber, Max. 1968 [1922]. *Economy and Society* (Gunther Roth and Claus Wittich, eds.). Berkeley, CA: University of California Press.

Weinstein, Jeremy M. 2005. "Autonomous Recovery and International Intervention in Comparative Perspective," Center for Global Development Working Paper No. 57. Available at: http://www.cgdev.org/files/2731_file_WP57.pdf.

Weiss, Thomas J. 2004. "The Humanitarian Impulse," in David M. Malone, ed., *The UN Security Council: From the Cold War to the 21st Century*. Boulder, CO: Lynne Rienner.

Weller, Marc and Stefan Wolff, eds. 2007. *Internationalized Statebuilding after Violent Conflict: Bosnia Ten Years after Dayton*. Abingdon: Routledge.

Wennman, Achim. 2011. *The Political Economy of Peacemaking*. Abingdon: Routledge.

Whaites, Alan. 2008. "States in Development: Understanding Statebuilding," London: Department for International Development.

Wheeler, Nicholas J. 2000. *Saving Strangers: Humanitarian Intervention in International Society*. Oxford: Oxford University Press.

Widner, Jennifer, 1995. "States and Statelessness in Late-Twentieth Century Africa," *Daedalus* 124 (3): 129–53.

Wittfogel, Karl. 1981. *Oriental Despotism: A Comparative Study of Total Power*. New York: Vintage Books.

Wolff, Stefan. 2003. *Disputed Territories: The Transnational Dynamics of Ethnic Conflict Settlement*. New York: Berghahn Books.

Wolpe, Howard and Steven MacDonald. 2008. "Democracy and Peacebuilding: Rethinking the Conventional Wisdom," *The Round Table* 97 (394): 137–45.

World Bank. 2011. *World Development Report 2011: Conflict, Security, and Development*. Washington, DC: World Bank. Available at: http://wdr2011.worldbank.org/fulltext.

Wyeth, Vanessa and Timothy D. Sisk (2009) "Rethinking Peacebuilding and State-building in Fragile and Conflict-Affected Countries: Conceptual Clarity, Policy Guidance and Practical Implications," Discussion Note for the OECD-DAC International Network on Conflict and Fragility.

Zartman, I. William, ed. 1995. *Collapsed States: The Disintegration and Restoration of Legitimate Authority*. Boulder, CO: Lynne Rienner.

Zartman, I. William. 2005. "Need, Creed, and Greed in Interstate Conflict," in Cynthia J. Arnson and I. William Zartman, eds., *Rethinking the Economics of War: The Intersection of Need, Creed, and Greed*. Washington, DC: The Woodrow Wilson Center Press.

Zaum, Dominik. 2007. *The Sovereignty Paradox: The Norms and Politics of International Statebuilding*. Oxford: Oxford University Press.

Zhao, Suisheng. 2004. *A Nation-State by Construction: Dynamics of Modern Chinese Nationalism*. Stanford, CA: Stanford University Press.

Zhou, Yongming. 1999. *Anti-Drug Crusades in Twentieth-century China: Nationalism, History, and Statebuilding*. Lanham, MD: Rowman and Littlefield.

Index